Hannes Gumtau
Wolfgang Kurschatke

Realschulabschluss Englisch

Prüfungsvorbereitung

MANZ VERLAG

2. verbesserte Auflage 2000
Manz Verlag

Lektorat: Harald Kotlarz, Ammerbuch
Umschlaggestaltung: Zembsch' Werkstatt, München
Illustrationen: Hans Limo Lechner, Pastetten
Layout: Hans Limo Lechner, Pastetten
Druck: Manz Druck GmbH, München
Printed in Germany

ISBN 3-7863-0595-1

5. Übersetzung — Translation

Wir wollen auf drei Fragen Antwort geben:

Was?
Wie?
Wo?

Was? Du erfährst, was in deiner Abschlussprüfung drankommen kann. Es ist sicher nicht genau dasselbe wie in unseren Beispielen. Vielleicht kommt nicht alles dran, was du in dieser Lernhilfe findest, auf alle Fälle kannst du dich intensiv vorbereiten.

Wie? Wir sagen dir bei allen Aufgaben, wie du vorgehen solltest, was du vermeiden solltest, wie du möglichst gute Ergebnisse erzielen kannst – in kürzester Zeit.

Wo? Wir bieten dir bei besonders wichtigen Aufgaben die nötigen Hintergrundinformationen direkt.
Du kannst dich in den *last minute-Übungen* noch in letzter Minute auf bestimmte Aufgaben vorbereiten.
Du findest in den Zusammenstellungen der *survival kits* alle wichtigen Lernstoffe, damit du sie schnell parat hast.

tipps&tricks

Lies den Text etwa dreimal durch.
Lass dir Zeit dabei:
Du hast 120 Minuten Arbeitszeit!

Versuche den gesamten Inhalt der Geschichte zu verstehen. Manche Fragen beziehen sich auf mehr als eine Textstelle. Du brauchst also einen guten Überblick.

Markiere Textstellen, bei denen du nicht so sicher bist. Vergeude nicht zu viel Zeit auf einzelne Wörter.
Wenn du die Aufgaben bearbeitest, wird dir allmählich manches klarer und einiges löst sich „von selbst".

Beachte die Zeilenangaben am linken Rand des Textes. Sie helfen dir, bestimmte Wörter oder Ausdrücke leichter zu finden.

Lass dir am Schluss etwas Zeit zum gründlichen „Durchchecken" aller Antworten, zum Schließen noch vorhandener Lücken und für das eine oder andere markierte Problemwort.

Viel Erfolg!

1. Comprehension Test

INFO

Beginne mit diesem Test, arbeite ihn gründlich durch. Vergleiche deine Lösungen mit den Antworten der Autoren. Notiere dir, wo du Schwächen hast, und arbeite anschließend die entsprechenden Kapitel im Buch durch.

California – The Broken Dream

"I was sleeping when the house started shaking. Was it a nightmare? I woke up scared to death. It was 4.31 a.m. My bed was being thrown around the room; a picture flew off the wall and almost hit me in the head. I thought I was dead."

The horror Sue Warner, a high school student, described for a local newspaper was shared by many in the early hours of January 17, 1994, when a big earthquake shook the second largest city in the U.S.A. The first quake, followed by smaller aftershocks, lasted just 30 to 40 seconds, but it did terrible damage. Windows were smashed, schools and apartment buildings were destroyed. Cars lay under the ruins of their garages. Gas lines exploded and caused big fires, the electricity was cut off, and many people were without water. Roads and bridges were damaged – a catastrophe for Los Angeles, whose highways are some of the busiest in the U.S.A. At least 60 people died and many more were seriously injured. There would probably have been more deaths if the earthquake had not happened on a public holiday, when fewer people than usual were on the roads.

Thousands were made homeless by the disaster. Some squeezed in with friends or relatives, others were evacuated to schools, parks and camps. Seventy-five of the city's 650 public schools were declared unsafe. What a way to earn an extra week's vacation!

California is generally known as the "Golden State" because in the last century gold was found there. It was once a symbol of the American Dream. Yet, it was also the "golden" sun and the beauty of the "golden" beaches which attracted people. They crossed the whole continent from east to west to settle along the coastline of the Pacific Ocean, at the foot of the high Sierra Nevada mountains. They did not worry about the earthquakes. This has changed, ever since scientists have been warning about the "Big One" – an earthquake even bigger than January's and as bad as the one in 1906, which destroyed San Francisco. Many Californians don't want to risk their lives waiting for this to happen. That's why since the 1980s people and especially the wealthy middle-class have been leaving California.

And the Golden State's natural disasters – earthquakes, floods and fires – are not its only problems. Man-made disasters have driven people away, too. Race problems, gang violence and poverty have increased lately, especially in a city whose founders named it "the angels". The state's economy has suffered in recent years as well. Since 1990, over 1 million jobs have been lost in California due to recession. Another problem is the great number of immigrants from Latin America and Asia, whom the state cannot afford to support and educate.
So it is easy to see why, for the first time, the population of some areas of California, particularly around Los Angeles, have stopped growing. Instead people are moving to Arizona, Oregon, Washington and Montana. Sue Warner, however, belongs to those people who know how to hide their fears. They live their lives and build their dreams on top of the earthquake fault lines*. "My family doesn't intend to leave," says Sue smilingly, "I wouldn't want to lose my friends, the warm climate, the lovely beaches and the beautiful canyons."

*fault line: a large crack in the earth along which earthquakes can occur

Complete the following sentences by using the information given in the text.

1. New York City has the largest population of all cities in the U.S.A.;

   Los Angeles . . . .

2. Although the earthquake lasted only half a minute, ...

   . . . .

3. In 1906 . . . .

4. The great number of immigrants has become a problem because . . . .

   . . . .

Use words of the same word family as the ones underlined to complete the sentences.

5. Sue Warner <u>lives</u> in L.A.; her . . . . was in danger when the earth started shaking.

6. More than 60 people <u>died</u>; some of them were found .... under a freeway that had collapsed.

7. Sue <u>described</u> her experience of the disaster to a reporter; her .... was printed in the local newspaper.

8. Sue wouldn't like to <u>lose</u> her friends, such a .... would hurt her too much.

Which words from the text fit best?

9. For many in L.A. the damage and destruction caused by the earthquake was a

....

10. Sue Warner .... the horror of the quake with her family, friends and neighbors.

11. All the people who lost their homes had to be evacuated and .... in with friends and relatives.

12. California's .... has weakened since 1990.

Paraphrase or replace the underlined expressions.

13. It was 4.32 <u>a.m.</u> (line 3)

....

14. L.A.'s highways are <u>some of the busiest</u> in the U.S. (line 15)

There ....

15. ... and more were <u>seriously injured.</u> (line 16)

....

16. ... people, <u>especially</u> the <u>wealthy</u> middle class, ... (line 30)

....

17. ... jobs have been lost ... <u>due to</u> recession. (line 36)

....

Explain the following words by finishing the sentences.

18. A nightmare (line 2) is ....

19. Immigrants (line 37) are ....

....

Answer the following questions on the text in complete sentences.

20. What happened in Sue's room during the earthquake? Give two items.

21. Why were there fewer people on the highways on January 17, 1994?

22. What makes California so sure that there will be more earthquakes to follow? Mention two facts. (Look at the map and the text)

23. Apart from natural disasters, why do some Californians move to other states? Name two reasons.

Additional tasks

24. Which American state, apart from California, would you like to visit and why?

25. Describe a natural disaster which can happen in Germany and its consequences.

26. What kind of violence can you find in our cities, and what should be done to reduce it?

Complete the text using the words in brackets in the correct form.
You may have to add words.

27. Ever since the earthquake in 1906 Californians (live) ....

in fear .... the "Big One". Small quakes, which make the earth tremble (slight) . . . . are common. It is also common that the residents, young and old, (be, teach) . . . . how (react). . . . . when a big earthquake (occur) . . . . Once in a year, on Earthquake Awareness Day, hospitals and emergency services practise what should (do) . . . . in the case of a quake.

For years safety regulations (work out). . . . . by experts.

Mr Warner, Sue's father, who is a scientist and an expert (oneself). . . . . expresses what many people, ... live near the fault lines, think: "If only we (can, forecast) . . . . natural disasters better! In any case, my family and I (stay) . . . . here, and we are looking forward (spend). . . . . our lives in the most beautiful state. . . . . the USA. Our house (build) . . . . by experts three years ago according to the (late). . . . . safety regulations, and it (cost) . . . . a lot of money. If these special regulations had also been applied to public buildings, more people (survive). . . . . the last quake. Now we must be (careful) . . . . than ever because the 'Big One' is bound to happen in the not . . . . distant future."

28. Last year you visited your cousin Martin, who is a student at Stanford University in California. You took some notes during the trip. Write an article for your school magazine in English.

– departure from Frankfurt, 5 p.m., July 31 . . . .

. . . .

. . . .

– Martin at San Francisco airport, arrival: 22.00 hours . . . .

. . . .

. . . .

– to Stanford, stay on university campus . . . .

. . . .

. . . .

– weekend, trip to San Francisco, about 40 miles . . . .

. . . .

. . . .

– cool, only 18°C . . . .

. . . .

. . . .

– souvenirs, night in a motel . . . .

. . . .

. . . .

29. It is important for every Californian to know how to reduce dangers.
– Look at the following signs and write down what a person must do or should avoid before, during and after an earthquake, and say why.

Before:

During:

After:

30. Translate into German:

The Richter Scale

The Richter scale shows how big an earthquake is, and the effects it can have. Here is what even young children in California are told:

Scale:

3.5-4.2 The quake is so slight that one can scarcely notice it.

4.3-4.8 Houses shake as if heavy trucks are going past. People wake up and church bells ring.

4.9-5.4 Trees start swinging. Loose objects* fall from shelves.

5.5-6.1 A general alarm goes off. Walls and ceilings are damaged.

6.2-6.9 Gas pipes explode. Chimneys and outer walls fall down.

7.0-7.3 Trains run off the rails. Bridges and tall buildings are destroyed, if they were not constructed properly.

7.4-8.1 Fires spread and may kill people. Cities are in ruins.

> 8.1 The surface of the earth moves in rising and falling waves, which causes total destruction.

*soll nicht mit dem Fremdwort übersetzt werden

1. Comprehension

INFO Lies den Text in Ruhe durch und suche dann eine Textstelle, die eine Aussage bestätigt *(a phrase from the text which tells you).*

Wisdom

A Scotsman went to see a doctor about his health. After the examination the doctor said, "What you are suffering from[1], my good Sir, is too much whisky drinking, and, if you don't give up at once, you will lose your sight"[2]. After a few weeks the man again visited the doctor and said he felt no better. "Have you given up drinking?" he was asked. "No," answered the man. "But you know that I warned you about blindness," said the doctor. "I know you did," replied the man, "but I'm just thinking that I've seen about all that's worth seeing."

[1] to suffer from (leiden unter)
[2] to lose one's sight (sein Augenlicht verlieren)

1 Write down the phrase from the text which tells you that ...

a) The Scotsman thought he was ill

. . . .

b) The man will go blind

. . . .

c) His health didn't improve

. . . .

d) The man didn't want to see anything else

. . . .

tipps&tricks Suche für die Aussagen eine andere Formulierung *(paraphrase)* im Text.
Auf den Seiten 32–35 findest du Aufgaben, bei denen du selbstständig paraphrasieren musst.

INFO

Lies den Text in Ruhe durch und finde die Textstellen, die du brauchst, um die angefangenen Sätze zu Ende zu schreiben *(finish the sentences using the information in the text).*

On the bus

There was no vacant seat on the bus, but as a good-looking woman entered, an elderly man near the door attempted to rise, but the lady at once forced him back into his seat. "Thank you," she said, "but please don't do that. I am perfectly able to stand."

"But, madam, allow ..." "I insist upon you keeping your seat," interrupted the woman with her hands on his shoulders. The man continued his efforts to stand up, saying, "Madam, will you kindly allow me to ... ..."With another push the woman forced him back, saying that she couldn't accept his seat. With a last effort the man pushed her aside. "Madam," he exclaimed, "you have already carried me three blocks beyond my destination. I don't care whether you take my seat or not, but I want to get off."

2 Finish the sentences using the information in the text.

a) The woman couldn't sit down because

. . . .

b) The elderly man tried to stand up when

. . . .

c) When he wanted to rise again, the woman

. . . .

d) She thought that the man wanted to

. . . .

tipps&tricks

Achte auf die grammatikalisch richtige Satzverknüpfung. So verwendest du bei a) *simple past* wie im Hauptsatz *the woman couldn't sit* oder bei d) den Infinitiv als Verbindung zu *the man wanted to ...*

INFO

Du sollst herausfinden, ob bestimmte Aussagen richtig oder falsch *(true or false)* sind, d. h. dem entsprechen, was im Text steht oder nicht.

Windsor Castle

Open daily throughout the year.
November – March 10.00-16.00
last *admission* 15.00
April – October 10.00-17.00
last admission 16.00.
Windsor Castle is a Royal Palace and opening arrangements are subject to change[1] at short notice.
For the latest information please telephone our 24 hour information line **01753 831118.**

[1]subject to change (Änderungen vorbehalten)

How to get there

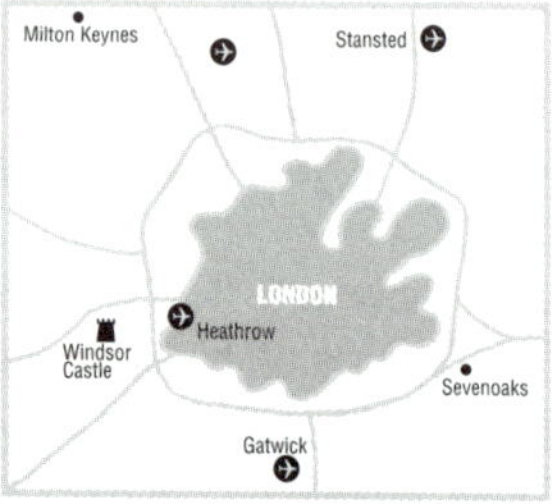

Situated 20 miles west of London, Windsor Castle is reached easily by train, car and coach.
By train – London Waterloo Station every 30 mins Mon-Sat and every hour on Sun. Telephone **0171-928 5100** for details.
By coach – Victoria Coach Station every 30 mins. Telephone **0181-668 7261** for details.

3 **Are these statements true or false according to the text? Put a cross in the correct box.**

	T	F
a) Tourists can visit Windsor Castle every day, even on Sundays.		
b) In winter Windsor Castle closes at 3 p.m.		
c) In summer visitors must leave the castle at 4 p.m.		
d) The opening hours may be changed.		
e) There are frequent trains from London to Windsor.		
f) Windsor Castle is near Gatwick Airport.		

tipps&tricks

Lies die Textstelle (aus einem Besucherprospekt für Windsor Castle) einige Male durch und kreuze dann das entsprechende Kästchen an *(Put a cross in the correct box).*

INFO

Auch hier sollst du herausfinden, ob gewisse Behauptungen *(statements)* dem Text entsprechen oder nicht. Entscheide dich und schreibe entweder *true (T) (richtig)* oder *false (F) (falsch)* hin.

How did they make Pinocchio's nose grow?

Walt Disney's team worked for nine whole months to produce the scene which lasts just two minutes on the screen. They started work on the film in 1935 and finished in 1939. Frank Thomas, one of the artists, explained how they made Pinocchio's nose grow. "All of us knew from the book how important the scene was, and we spent about a week deciding how long the nose should be, what it should look like, and so on." The story team took about two months to draw the original ideas. "Initially his nose was a straight, wooden beam[1], but that looked boring, so someone suggested making it grow leaves. Two hundred drawings later, the bird's nest was added, and finally, Pinocchio told his last lie, we made it return to normal." If Disney himself liked the ideas they were sent on for animation. After endless improvements and changes, the thousands of pictures were brought to life by five artists for camera filming, which took about six months.

[1] beam (Balken)

4 Are these statements true or false, according to the text? Write true or false.

	T	F
a) After nine months the team had created the two-minute scene.		
b) The film only took three years to make.		
c) It took about seven days to decide on the size and shape of the nose.		
d) These initial ideas were drawn over the following two weeks.		
e) First of all the nose had leaves on it.		
f) Some time later the nose was given a bird's nest too.		
g) Walt Disney did not need to check the ideas.		
h) Five artists filmed the thousands of pictures.		

INFO Lies den Text in Ruhe durch (am besten mit einem Lineal als Unterlage), entscheide dann, ob die Aussagen stimmen oder nicht und füge zum Beweis die entsprechenden Sätze/Satzteile aus dem Text an *(write down the corresponding sentences from the text).*

Crisis at Christmas.

"Crisis[1] at Christmas," an organisation which helps homeless people at this time of the year, expects to be looking after about 1,000 of London's 3,000 street people during the holiday, twice as many as in 1980. "There will be a lot more young people than there were ten years ago," a worker for the charity[2], now in its 25th year, said. "The churches we use as temporary shelters, are too small and offer too few facilities. We need somewhere that offers plenty of electricity and hot water." The homeless will be provided with hot showers and the services of hairdressers, dentists and doctors. The shelter stays open throughout the Christmas week when the usual refuges[3] from the cold – libraries, Tube stations and various day centres – are closed. About ten years ago these would largely be people who had dropped out[4]. Now, a lot of them want to succeed in society, but cannot find anywhere affordable to live.

1 crisis (Krise) 2 charity (karitative Organisation) 3 refuge (Zuflucht) 4 drop out (aussteigen)

5 Are these statements true or false?
Write down the corresponding sentences from the text.

a) The organisation helps people all the year round.

That's .... because it says in the text ....

b) In 1980 the charity cared for about 500 people.

c) They are not allowed to use churches as shelters.

d) The churches are big enough.

e) The homeless can have their hair cut at the shelter.

INFO

Du sollst Fragen zum Text *(questions on the text)* in vollständigen Sätzen beantworten *(answer in complete sentences)*. Du bemühst dich um möglichst eigene Formulierungen *(use your own words)*, um eine hohe Punktezahl zu erreichen.

A Visit to Australia

In 1978 John's elder sister emigrated to Australia. Three years later she got married and today she has two children aged eight and six. Since the air fare for the whole family was too expensive, John's parents had never seen their grandchildren until a few months ago.

Just before Christmas, however, John's father won £ 10,000 in the Football Pools, and he decided that they should all visit Australia. John's mother had never flown before and the nearer the day of their departure came the more frightened she became. But John's father finally succeeded in reassuring[1] her. He said, "Just think! We've been sending air-mail letters to our daughter every week for so many years and not a single one has ever been lost on the way!"

1 reassure (beruhigen)

6 Answer in complete sentences using your own words.

a) Where does John's sister live now?

b) In what year did she get married?

c) How old is her youngest child?

d) Why couldn't John's parents travel to Australia?

e) Was John's mother fond of flying? Give reasons for your answer.

f) How did John's father manage to reassure his wife?

tipps&tricks

Lies den Text zwei- bis dreimal durch, um den Zusammenhang zu verstehen, und suche erst dann die betreffenden Textstellen. Achte vor allem auf die richtige Wortstellung und darauf, dass die Zeiten in Frage und Antwort übereinstimmen, z. B. a) *Where does ... live*? → She *lives* ...

INFO Lies den Text konzentriert mehrmals durch, um den Inhalt zu verstehen. Beantworte dann die Fragen in vollständigen Sätzen.

The Hammer

The cement mixers used on modern building sites are complicated and sensitive pieces of equipment, so it was a catastrophe when a worker dropped his hammer into one. First they tried to fish it out with a long pair of tongs[1], but in vain. So the whole machine had to be taken apart and as they did so, they found that the mechanism was broken. Since there were no spare parts available, the workers had to be sent home and work was halted for several days. All this meant a loss of thousands of pounds for the building firm. So, as soon as the repair was finished the hammer was returned to the careless worker and he was sacked[2] on the spot. “Well, I don’t need that any more,” said the worker, throwing the hammer back into the cement mixer.

1 a pair of tongs (eine Zange)
2 to sack (entlassen)

7 Answer in complete sentences.

a) Where are cement mixers used today?

b) What did the worker do to cause such a trouble?

c) How did they try to get the hammer out of the cement mixer?

d) Why were the workers sent home?

e) How much money did the building firm lose?

f) Why was the worker sacked?

g) What did he do with the hammer before he left?

tipps&tricks

Achte auf die genaue Bedeutung der Fragewörter *(Where? What? How? Why?)*

Auf die Frage *Why – Warum*? kannst du nicht einfach mit “*Because* ...” antworten, denn du sollst ja vollständige Sätze schreiben. Schreibe also **nicht** d) *Because there were no spare parts available,* **sondern** *There were no spare parts available* **oder:** *They were sent home because there were no spare parts available.*

Achte auch darauf, dass sich die Zeiten in Frage und Antwort entsprechen, z. B. a) *Where are they used?* → *They are used* ... (simple present passive).

INFO

Lies die Geschichte sorgfältig durch und beantworte die Fragen. Die Antworten können weitgehend aus dem Text übernommen werden, denn es soll ja vor allem das Leseverstehen überprüft werden. Es fehlt die Angabe "*Use your own words*".

Robinson Crusoe's House

I soon found the place I was in was not for my settlement, especially because it was upon a low moorish[1] ground near the sea. I thought that it would not be healthy there, because there was no fresh water near it. So I decided to find a more healthy and finer spot of ground. I thought of several things which were necessary for me. First, health and fresh water. Secondly, shelter from the heat of the sun. Thirdly, safety from wild creatures, whether men or beast. Fourthly, a view to the sea, that if God sent any ship near the island, I would have the opportunity to get away from here.

When I looked for a place as I imagined, I found a little plain on the side of a hill which had a steep rocky slope with a hollow[2] in it. It looked like a small cave and perhaps I could make it deeper and put all my stores in it. On the flat, grassy place, just before this hollow, I decided to pitch my tent. Around this little spot I built a fence. Then I took my sledge-hammer[3] and an iron bar and started to make the cave in the rock larger. The next important thing was to make a roof. From the ship I had brought large pieces of sailcloth and I fixed these to the posts of a palisade. When this was finished, I had at least a protection against the weather.

Now I am tired, and I want to sleep, but there are still many things to do which I need in my house.

1 moorish (Moor-) 2 hollow (Vertiefung) 3 sledge-hammer (Vorschlaghammer)

8 **Answer in complete sentences.**

a) For which reason did Robinson not think the low ground was suitable?

b) How many things did he think were necessary?

c) What would he need for drinking?

d) Why did Robinson want a view of the sea?

e) How was he going to use the flat, grassy place?

f) Where had he got the large pieces of sailcloth from?

tipps&tricks

Schreibe vollständige Sätze *(answer in complete sentences)*. Vokabel- und Grammatikfehler sowie Verstöße gegen die englische Schreibweise führen zu Punktabzug. Bei einer inhaltlich falschen Antwort entfallen **alle** Punkte.

WHITE HOUSE 1600 Pennsylvania Ave. NW, Washington, DC 20500. (202) 456-2322. The official residence of the president of the United States. Free guided tours Tuesday-Saturday 10 a.m.-noon. Tickets required[1] spring and summer; tickets are valid[2] only on the day issued[3] (no advance tickets). Ticket line forms on the Ellipse on the south side of the White House. Plan to arrive early; tickets may be gone as early as 8:30 a.m. All tours subject to change and cancellation[4] for private White House functions. For the latest schedule[5], call White House Visitor Office recorded information lines: (202) 456-2200 (special events) or (202) 456-7041 (tours).

1 to require (benötigen)
2 valid (gültig)
3 to issue (ausgeben)
4 subject to cancellation (Absagen vorbehalten)
5 schedule (Zeitplan, Programm)

9 Answer in complete sentences.

a) What's the official residence of the president of the United States called?

b) In which city is it?

c) When can people visit the White House?

d) Why is it no use buying tickets a few days before a planned visit?

e) Why are visitors asked to come early in the morning?

tipps&tricks

Antworte in vollständigen Sätzen. Beginne keine Antwort mit *"Because ..."*.

Achte vor allem auf die Fragewörter *(What is called? In which? When? Why?)* und die Übereinstimmung der Zeiten in Frage und Antwort, z. B. a) What's *it called* ... → *It is called* ... b) When *can* people *visit* ... → They *can visit* ... .

Fragewörter		fragt nach ...
How?	*Wie?*	... der **Art und Weise** bzw. ... dem **Mittel.**
How long?	*Wie lange?*	... der **Dauer.**
How much?	*Wie viel?*	... nach der **Menge (Singular)**.
How many?	*Wie viele?*	... der **Anzahl (Plural)**.
How often?	*Wie oft?*	... nach der **Häufigkeit**.
What?	*Was?*	... nach **Sachen, Ursachen** bzw. **Handlungen.**
What?	*Was für?*	
What kind of?	*Was für ein?*	
What ... like?	*Wie ist ... denn?*	
What ... for?	*Wofür?*	
When?	*Wann?*	... nach der **Zeit.**
Where?	*Wo?* *Wohin?*	... nach dem **Ort.** ... nach der **Richtung.**
Which? **Which of you?**	*Welches?* *Wer von euch?*	... nach **Personen oder Sachen. aus einer bestimmten Zahl.**
Who?	*Wer?* *Wen?*	... nach **Personen im Subjekt** (Wer?) **bzw. Objekt** (Wen?)
Whom?	*Wen?*	... nach **Personen im Objekt.**
Whose? **Whose is it?**	*Wessen?* *Wem gehört es?*	... nach dem **Besitzer** bzw. der **Zugehörigkeit.**
Why?	*Warum?*	... nach dem **Grund oder Zweck.**

Fragen	mögliche Antworten
How does Tom drive?	He drives **carefully.**
How does Susan get to school?	She gets to school **by bike.**
How long did you wait?	We waited **over an hour.**
How much time have we got?	We've got **an hour.**
How many people did you see?	I saw **about ten people.**
How often do you go to the club?	**Twice a week.**
What happened to Jason?	I don't know.
What do you know about Jane?	She's on holiday.
What films do you like?	Cowboy films.
What kind of car have you got?	A van.
What is Peter **like**?	He's **tall and friendly**.
What do you need this **for**?	For **the bus.**
When can we meet?	At **five o'clock**.
	On **Monday**.
	In **July**/In **summer**/In **1998.**
	On **24th March**.
Where did you meet Geoff?	At **Manchester**.
	In **Scotland**.
Where did Geoff go?	To **Ireland**.
Which book did you buy?	The red one.
Which of you knows the answer?	Jane.
Who reads comics?	Ian./**Ian does**.
Who did you meet last night?	Geoff. I met Geoff.
Whom did you meet last night?	
Whose bike is over there?	**Peter's** bike./**My** bike./**Mine**.
Whose is it?	
Why do you smoke?	**I'm nervous** and it helps me.
	I smoke **because I'm nervous**.

Du sollst zu bestimmten Sachverhalten (die sich inhaltlich auf einen Prüfungstext beziehen) deine Meinung sagen. Da häufig eine hohe Punktezahl zu erreichen ist, solltest du komplexere Antworten schreiben.

INFO

10 **Say whether you agree or disagree with the following statements and give a reason for your answer.**

a) Men should wear ties in banks and offices.

....

....

....

b) Doc Martens are too large and heavy for girls.

....

....

....

c) I can print whatever I want on my T-shirt.

....

....

....

tipps&tricks

Lies die Fragen genau! Du musst dich entscheiden, ob du mit der Behauptung übereinstimmst *(you agree)* oder anderer Meinung bist *(or disagree)*; du musst in jedem Falle eine Begründung angeben *(and give a reason for your answer).* Du könntest z. B. anfangen mit *I think so because ...* .

INFO

Du sollst Fragen, die über den Text hinausgehen *(further questions or additional questions)*, in vollständigen Sätzen beantworten *(answer in complete sentences)*. Die Lösungen kannst du nicht aus dem Text entnehmen, du musst deine eigene Meinung auf Englisch ausdrücken. Oft musst du auch eine persönliche Begründung für deine Antwort finden. Unter 11) wird nach dem Grund gefragt *(why)*, bei 12) musst du drei Gründe angeben *(give three reasons)*.

11 **Which part of Great Britain would you like to visit, and why? Write two complete sentences.**

. . . .

. . . .

. . . .

. . . .

12 **Why do so many foreigners come to London? Write complete sentences, giving three reasons.**

. . . .

. . . .

. . . .

. . . .

tipps&tricks

Gehe auf alle Teile der Fragen ein, damit du möglichst viele Punkte erhältst.

Hier einige Übungshilfen:

11) *Wales, Highlands of Scotland, Midlands, Cornwall → hiking in the mountains, beautiful scenery, coast and beaches, old villages and towns*

12) *sights (such as the Tower, Buckingham Palace, Westminster Abbey), museums (Madame Tussaud's, Natural Science Museum), shopping (Harrods, Selfridges), practise English (language school, youth hostel, bed and breakfast).*

13 **What is the advantage of having an underground railway system? Write complete sentences. Give two reasons.**

. . . .

. . . .

. . . .

14 **What are the advantages and disadvantages of "fast food"? Write complete sentences. Give a reason each.**

. . . .

. . . .

. . . .

15 **Which American state, apart from California, would you like to visit, and why? Write complete sentences.**

. . . .

. . . .

. . . .

tipps&tricks

Antworte in vollständigen Sätzen und achte auf die richtige Wortstellung. Berücksichtige die Zusatzfrage, um keinen Punktabzug zu riskieren: 13) ***two** reasons* – ***zwei*** Gründe; 14) *give a reason each* – gebe je einen Grund an, d. h. je einen Vorteil *(advantage)* und einen Nachteil *(disadvantage);* 15) ***apart from** California* – ***außer*** Kalifornien. Solltest du also über Kalifornien schreiben, verlierst du alle Punkte, auch wenn deine Antwort sprachlich gelungen war.

Begründungen – Meinungen – Vorschläge

Du sagst deine Meinung:	I think	*ich meine*
	I believe	*ich glaube*
	I feel	*ich finde*
	I don't think	*ich glaube nicht*
	In my opinion	*meiner Meinung nach*
	In my view	
	it seems to me	*es scheint mir*
	I'm convinced	*ich bin überzeugt*
Du stimmst zu:	I agree	*ich stimme zu*
	I agree with	*ich stimme mit…überein*
	Yes, of course	*Ja, natürlich*
	Yes, that's right	*Ja, das stimmt*
	Yes, that's true	*Ja, das ist wahr*
	Yes, exactly	*Ja, genau (so ist es)*
	I think so, too	*Das denke ich auch*
	Certainly	*Gewiss*
	Indeed	*In der Tat*
Du widersprichst:	I'm afraid I don't agree/I disagree	*Ich kann leider nicht zustimmen*
	I would say that	*Ich würde sagen, dass*
	on the contrary	*im Gegenteil*
	it's impossible	*es ist unmöglich*
	I can't accept that	*Das kann ich nicht annehmen*

survival Kit

Begründungen – Meinungen – Vorschläge

Du schlägst vor:

We could ...	Wir könnten ...
Let's ...	Lasst uns ...
Why don't we ...?	Warum ... nicht ...?
What about ...?	Wie wär's, wenn ...?
I suggest ...	Ich schlage vor ...

Du begründest etwas:

... because	... weil
As/Since ...	Da/Weil ...
It is because of ...	Es ist wegen ...
It is due to ...	Es ist aufgrund ...

Du bist sicher:

I'm sure	Ich bin sicher
I'm certain	
Certainly	Gewiss, sicherlich

Du weißt etwas nicht:

I don't know	Ich weiß nicht
I've no idea	Ich habe keine Ahnung
I'm not sure	Ich bin nicht sicher
Perhaps/	
Maybe ...	Vielleicht ...

2. Vocabulary

INFO Lies den Text (Prospekt zum Besuch des Londoner Wembley Stadions) genau durch. Ersetze dann einige der Wörter durch Synonyme *(replace the underlined words with synonyms)*. Synonyme sind Wörter mit (fast) derselben Bedeutung.

Please Note

Tours leave promptly on the hour, so please allow sufficient time to get to Wembley.

Special facilities[1] can be made available for the disabled. If you wish to arrange an organised visit, please inform us at least three weeks in advance, so that adequate[2] preparation can be made. It should be noted however, that as there are many steps at the Stadium, these could be inconvenient for elderly or handicapped people.

1 facilities (Einrichtungen) 2 adequate (angemessen)

How to get to Wembley

By Road

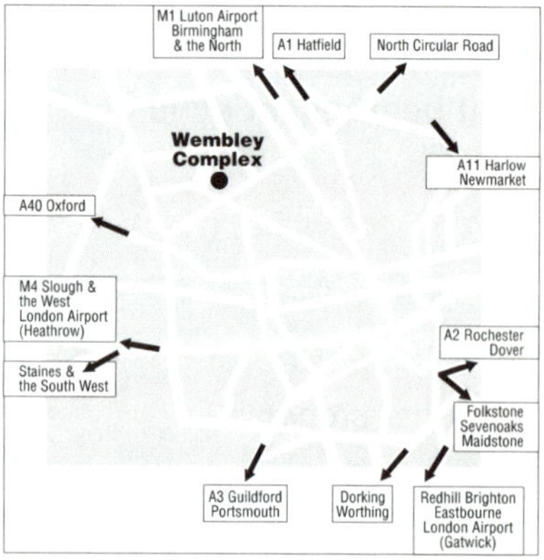

1 Replace these words with synonyms. Your friend doesn't understand some words of the text.

a) promptly . . . .

b) sufficient . . . .

c) to wish . . . .

d) in advance . . . .

e) to get to . . . .

f) by road . . . .

tipps&tricks Achte vor allem auf die Wortart, die übereinstimmen muss, z. B. a) Adverb *promptly,* b) Adjektiv *sufficient*, c) Verb *to wish*

2 Find words with the same meaning.

a) They **own** a house in Greenwich.
b) They want to **purchase a** new car.
c) There was **sufficient** time.
d) The lesson was **dull.**
e) I couldn't **persuade** Tom to go.
f) Susan is **glad.**
g) We can't **allow** this.

h) Don't **ruin** the wall.
i) Donkeys **pull** little carts.
j) Can you **finish** the sentence?
k) I hope I'll **get** a letter.

l) Paul **nearly** scored a goal.
m) This place is **ideal.**
n) Can you **mend** my bike?
o) I met all **sorts** of people.
p) Jane bought a **valuable** necklace.
q) I ask and you **reply.**
r) Mr Corn has a **big** farm.

INFO

Lies den Text (Prospekt für eine bekannte Londoner Sehenswürdigkeit) genau durch, um den Inhalt zu verstehen. Ersetze dann die unterstrichenen Wörter *(words)* bzw. Ausdrücke *(expressions)* durch eigene Formulierungen. Manchmal genügt es auch, wenn du ein Synonym findest (Dies ist häufig der Fall, wenn nur 1 Punkt für die Antwort angeführt ist!).

MADAME TUSSAUD'S

BAKER STREET • LONDON

★ Madame Tussaud's is open from 10am to 5.30pm every day except Christmas Day.
★ Doors open earlier every weekend, on Bank Holidays and during the Summer Season.
★ Admission[1] prices include VAT[2].
★ Children 4 years and under admitted free.
★ Souvenir Shop. ★ Combined tickets for Madame Tussaud's and the London Planetarium are available at a reduced rate[3]. ★ Discounts for groups of 10 or more. Apply to: Group Booking Office, Madame Tussaud's, Marylebone Road, London NW1 5LR. **Telephone: 0 71-9 35 68 61** ★ Promenade Pier Café – tea, coffee, hot and cold buffet. ★ Souvenir Photographs available. ★ Personal photography encouraged.

1 admission (Eintritt)
2 rate (Gebühr)
3 VAT= (value-added tax) (Mehrwertsteuer)

3 Paraphrase the underlined words or expressions or give a synonym.

a) They **are admitted** free ...

b) Combined tickets **are available** ...

c) **apply to:** Group Booking Office ...

d) it is open every day **except** Christmas ...

tipps&tricks

Zerlege die Ausdrücke in ihre Sinnteile und umschreibe sie dann in einfachen Worten, z. B. a) they **are admitted free** (*sie werden frei eingelassen* → sie dürfen kommen/das Haus betreten, ohne zu zahlen), b) tickets **are available** (*Eintrittskarten sind zu haben* → man kann die Karten kaufen), c) **apply to** *(wende dich an)* → hier fällt dir vielleicht ein Synonym ein, z. B. rufe an ..., schreibe an ...

4 Find the best explanations.

They are ...

a) busy
b) deaf
c) honest
d) hungry
e) lazy
f) patient
g) popular
h) punctual
i) tired
j) unemployed

They ...

1 are liked by lots of people
2 have a lot to do.
3 can't hear.
4 are on time.
5 must eat.
6 don't tell lies.
7 should sleep.
8 are without a job.
9 are unwilling to work.
10 are willing to wait.

5 Which are the paraphrases?

a) I owe/ ... Barbara £ 100.
b) Mr Fox deals in/ ... cars.
c) Geoff guides/ ... the visitors.
d) The road is well maintained/ ...
e) Some girls sometimes blush/ ...
f) Can you solve/ ... the problem
g) All passengers survived/ ...
h) The car is approaching/ ... the house.
i) They ignored/ ... the warning.
j) Why do you object to/ ... this?

1 stayed alive
2 shows round
3 have to pay back
4 are you against
5 is in a good condition
6 buys and sells
7 paid no attention to
8 find an answer to
9 become red in the face
10 is coming nearer to

tipps&tricks

Du solltest den Wortinhalt der Verben in seine Einzelbedeutungen zerlegen und dann in einfachen Worten wiedergeben, z. B. a) *I **owe** her money (Ich schulde ihr Geld → Ich muss ihr Geld zurückzahlen).*

6 **Some more exercises:**
Paraphrase the words in bold print.

a) The Wilsons **are abroad.**

. . . .

b) Jane Wilson **is blind.**

. . . .

c) She works in an office where she **is a reliable secretary.**

. . . .

d) Jane **invited** lots of people to her birthday party.

. . . .

e) Tom Wilson often **looks after** his grandma.

. . . .

f) He would like to have a new car, but he **can't afford it.**

. . . .

g) Jane was sad, she **dropped** a beautiful vase.

. . . .

tipps&tricks

Bei Aufgaben, in denen paraphrasiert werden soll, dürfen Präpositionen oder andere Strukturwörter grundsätzlich wiederverwendet werden. Auch sind Ableitungen innerhalb einer Wortfamilie erlaubt, z. B. reliable – to *rely* on. Du darfst also schreiben: a) The Wilsons (oder: They) *are* in ... country; c) Everyone in *the office* can ... on her/her work. Für einfache Umschreibungen ist im Allgemeinen 1 Punkt vorgesehen. Wenn mehr als 1 Punkt angegeben ist, solltest du eine umfangreiche Formulierung überlegen.

Lies den Abschnitt des Textes *Learning to baby-sit* aufmerksam durch und schreibe dann jeweils 2 Sätze, in denen du 2 verschiedene Bedeutungen der Wörter *while*, *change* und *way* aufzeigst.

INFO

Learning to Baby-Sit

No longer can it be taken for granted that a grandmother will take over the task of baby-sitting, **while** mother and father go to a dinner-party. The baby-sitter's amateur status has **changed** in the past four decades. Nowadays baby-sitting can be a regular job for those who want to improve their low incomes. This is where teenagers and university students step in. They are hired for the evening and expect to be paid on an hourly basis. Baby-sitting may seem a good **way** of earning some extramoney.

7 **Form two sentences each in order to show the two different meanings of the words "while" (l. 2), "change" (l. 3), and "way" (l. 6). Don't copy the sentences.**

while:

a) ....

b) ....

change:

a) ....

b) ....

way:

a) ....

b) ....

tipps&tricks

Schreibe zu jedem der drei Wörter zwei Sätze *(two sentences)*. Wenn du nur vom Text abschreibst, kannst du nicht mit der vollen Punktzahl rechnen. Überlege dir als erstes die Wortart, z. B. Verb, Substantiv, Konjunktion.

INFO

Finde zwei unterschiedliche Bedeutungen von ***fine*** bzw. ***fit*** mithilfe der kopierten Seiten aus einem Lexikon*. Berücksichtige, dass *fine* einmal als *Adjektiv* und einmal als Substantiv, *fit* einmal als *Adjektiv* und einmal als *Verb* gefordert werden.

8 **Show two different meanings of the following words: "fine" and "fit".**

a) fine:

as an adjective: . . . .

as a noun: . . . .

b) fit:

as an adjective: . . . .

as a verb: . . . .

fine[1]/fam/*Adj* **1** (*nur vor Nomen*) hochwertige, fein, gut **a fine piece of work** eine ausgezeichnete Arbeit **Rubens' finest painting** das beste Bild von Rubens
2 ausreichend, gut **Don't cook anything special – a sandwich will be fine.** Koch nichts Besonderes, ein Sandwich ist völlig ausreichend.
3 (*gesundheitlich*) gut **"How are you?" "Fine thanks".** „Wie geht es Ihnen?" „Danke gut!" **"Do you want to change places?" "No, I'm fine here, thanks."** „Willst du den Platz wechseln?" „Nein danke, ich sitze gut hier."
☛**Fine** in den Bedeutungen 2 und 3 kann nicht in Fragen oder verneinten Sätzen vorkommen. Sätze wie "Are you fine?" oder "This isn't fine" sind nicht möglich.
4 (*Wetter*) schön, trocken
5 fein **a fine pencil** ein feiner Bleistift

fine[2]/fam/*Nomen* Geldstrafe **You'll get a fine if you park here.** Wenn du hier parkst, bekommst du einen Strafzettel. **He'll have to pay a heavy fine.** Er muss eine hohe Strafe zahlen.

fine[3]/fam/*Verb* + *Obj* zu einer Geldstrafe verurteilen

fit[1]/fit/*Adj.* **(fitter, fittest) 1 fit for sb/sth** für jdn/etwas geeignet **fit to do sth** geeignet, etwas zu tun **These houses are not fit to live in.** Diese Häuser sind nicht zum Wohnen geeignet.
2 gesund, (körperlich) fit **He keeps fit by jogging.** Er hält sich durch Joggen fit. **She isn't fit for work yet.** Sie ist noch nicht arbeitsfähig. **keep-fit classes** Fitness-Kurse

fit[2]/fit/*Verb* (fi**tt**ing, fi**tt**ed, fi**tt**ed) **1** passen (auf, in) **This dress doesn't fit me any more.** Dieses Kleid passt mir nicht mehr. **This key doesn't fit the lock.** Dieser Schlüssel passt nicht ins Schloss.
2 unterbringen **Can you fit one more person in the car?** Passt noch einer mehr in das Auto? **I can't fit all these books onto the shelf.** Die Bücher passen nicht alle in das Regal.
3 anbringen **The builders are fitting new windows today.** Die Bauarbeiter setzen heute neue Fenster ein.
4 entsprechen; passen auf **The punishment should fit the crime.** Die Strafe sollte dem Verbrechen angemessen sein.
• **fit in (with sb/sth)** sich leicht (bei jdm/etwas) einfügen **I'll try to fit in with your plans.** Ich versuche, mich deinen Plänen anzupassen. **fit sb/sth** in für etwas/jdn Zeit finden. **The doctor managed to fit me in this morning.** Der Arzt konnte heute Morgen noch einen Termin für mich einschieben.

* *Das Oxford Schulwörterbuch*
English-German
Deutsch-Englisch
Oxford University Press, 1996

INFO

Du sollst die Wörter erklären, indem du die angefangenen Sätze zu Ende schreibst *(Explain ... by completing the sentences).*

9 **Explain the following words by completing the sentence.**

a) The National Gallery! – What's that?

It's a . . . where you can see . . .

b) Westminster Abbey! – What's that?

It's a . . . where . . .

c) Harrods! – What's that?

It's a . . . . where you can buy . . .

tipps&tricks

Wir empfehlen dir dieses Muster: ... *is a building/museum/shop/church/castle/place/ ... + where you can ... +* **typische Information.**

10 **Some more places.**

a) A booking-office is ...
b) A post office is ...
c) A railway station is ...
d) A telephone box is ...
e) A theatre is ...
f) A zoo is ...
g) A bus stop is ...
h) A coffee bar is ...
i) A pub is ...
j) A filling station

1 you can send letters and parcels
2 animals are kept
3 petrol and oil are sold
4 sweets and juice are served
5 tickets can be booked
6 trains arrive and leave
7 everyone can telephone
8 you can meet friends and have a drink
9 you can get on and off a bus
10 plays are performed

Of course, our shoes and boots have been copied again and again. These imitations look similar; only when you wear them you realise that they are not the same. You will soon find out how well the real "DMs"* protect your feet from the cold, mud and snow. Their soft leather and thick rubber soles are unbeatable.

* Doc Martens

11 **Explain the following words by finishing the sentence.**

a) A boot (l. 1) is ... .

b) Mud (l. 5) is ....

c) Leather (l. 6) is ... .

d) Rubber (l. 6) is ....

tipps&tricks

Du könntest etwas über das Aussehen, die Herkunft oder den Verwendungszweck sagen und dies mit einem Oberbegriff verbinden, z. B.
a) A boot is a ... *shoe.* – b) Mud is ... ... *earth.* – c) Leather is *made from ... of an animal.* – d) Rubber is *used for the ... of motorcars.*

12 **Some more definitions.**

a)	A by-pass	1	a room for coats and hats
b)	history	2	an area of land where there is little rain
c)	A cloakroom	3	meat from a pig's leg
d)	A commercial	4	the study of the past
e)	A compartment	5	pain in the head
f)	A desert	6	an advertisement on radio or TV
g)	The environment	7	a journey in a plane
h)	A flight	8	a road round the town or village
i)	ham	9	part of a railway carriage
j)	headache	10	the air, water and land around us

JOKE

Teacher: *"Can anyone define 'teacher' for me?"*
Geoff: *"Someone who talks in your sleep."*

13 **Define the following words in complete sentences.**

a) A teacher is someone who . . . .

b) A pupil is a boy or a girl . . . .

c) A rock star is a singer whose songs . . . .

tipps&tricks

Für Personen schlagen wir dieses Muster vor: ... *is someone* bzw. **Oberbegriff** *who (that)* ... (... ist jemand, der ...) ... *is someone* bzw. **Oberbegriff** *whose* ... (... ist jemand, dessen ...) + **typische Tätigkeit** oder **besonderes Merkmal.** Schreibe bitte keine Allerweltssätze, wie z. B. *A teacher is someone who works (reads, ...).*

d) A school is a building in which . . . .

e) A satchel is a small bag in which . . . .

f) A piece of chalk is something with which . . . .

tipps&tricks

Für andere Substantive (Sachen, Begriffe) empfehlen wir dieses Muster:
... *is something* bzw. **Oberbegriff** *which (that)* ...
... *is something* bzw. **Oberbegriff** *in/with which* ...
+ **sachdienliche Information** (z. B. Was geschieht dort? Was macht man damit?)

14 Who are they?

a) An apprentice is a young person
b) A businesswoman is a woman
c) A butcher is a man
d) A crew is a group of people
e) A dentist is a doctor
f) An employee is someone
g) An employer is someone
h) A grocer is a man or woman
i) A guide is a man or woman
j) A newsagent is a man or woman

1 repairs bad teeth
2 shows you the sights of a town
3 sells flour, coffee, tea and tins
4 works for a firm
5 is learning his or her job
6 sells meat and sausages
7 sells newspapers and magazines
8 work on a ship or plane
9 gives work to others
10 runs a business

15 What is it?

a) An album
b) A saw
c) A crane
d) A mirror
e) A skirt
f) Earth
g) A submarine
h) A calculator
i) A fine
j) A fare

1 a ship that can move under water
2 a counting machine that fits in your pocket
3 money (that) you pay as a punishment
4 money (that) you have to pay on the bus
5 one of the planets that move around our sun
6 a book in which photos or stamps can be placed
7 a piece of clothing that girls or women wear
8 a tall machine that can lift heavy objects
9 a piece of glass that you look into
10 a tool with which you can cut wood

INFO

Lies den Text genau durch und ersetze dann die unterstrichenen Wörter durch solche mit entgegengesetzter Bedeutung (*opposite* oder auch *antonym*).

School

Miss Jones had the laziest class in school. No matter how[1] hard she tried to make her lessons exciting she was met with complete apathy[2]. One day she came in and said, "As we've been learning French all term, I'm going to take you all for a day trip to Calais tomorrow. Hands up those who want to go. I'm paying."

Slowly, very slowly, the hands went up – except for Alec's.

"Alec, why haven't you raised your hand?"

"Too much effort, Miss."

1 no matter how (ganz egal wie) 2 apathy (Teilnahmslosigkeit)

16 Fill in the opposites.

a) Miss Jones tried to make her lessons exciting (l. 2),

but her pupils found them . . . .

b) The hands went up slowly (l. 6), but when the lesson was over the pupils

left the classroom . . . .

c) First the hands went up (l. 6), then they went . . . . again.

d) Alec didn't show much (l. 8) effort, he had only. . . . . interest in school.

tipps&tricks

Die Zeilenangaben (*line* – Zeile) helfen dir, die Wörter schnell im Text zu finden. Es ist wichtig, dass du den Zusammenhang verstehst, weil manche Wörter ja in verschiedenen Bedeutungen verwendet werden können. Achte auf die **Wortart** (Adjektiv, Adverb, Präposition etc.) und die **Form** (-ing, Singular/Plural, Zeit).

17 **Some more exercises:
Find verbs with the opposite meaning:**

a) hate
b) shout
c) export
d) remember
e) ask
f) lose
g) collect
h) fail

i) give
j) begin
k) defend
l) open
m) borrow
n) sell
o) forbid

JOKE

"You're ugly!"
"And you're drunk!"
"Yes, but in the morning I'll be sober, but you'll still be ugly."

18 **Find the opposites for these adjectives.**

a) dark	1 late
b) wide	2 beautiful
c) cheap	3 weak
d) short	4 high
e) early	5 narrow
f) true	6 long
g) ugly	7 false
h) closed	8 open
i) strong	9 thin
j) fat	10 bright
k) low	11 last
l) first	12 expensive

19 **Find the opposites for these nouns.**

a) consumer	1 failure
b) employer	2 victory
c) happiness	3 strength
d) noise	4 war
e) defeat	5 arrival
f) poverty	6 producer
g) success	7 divorce
h) peace	8 disagreement
i) weakness	9 silence
j) departure	10 misery
k) marriage	11 employee
l) agreement	12 wealth

20 Fill in words with opposite meaning.

a) Susan was **happy** yesterday, but today she's very . . . .

b) In the morning Peter **loaded** the boxes on the van, in the evening he helped his father to . . . . them again.

c) I can't **agree** with this plan. I . . . . with your proposal.

d) "Open" is a **regular** verb; but "go" is an . . . . verb.

e) Long legs are an **advantage** to a basketball player, but they are a . . . . to a football player.

f) This exercise isn't **useful;** it is absolutely . . . .

tipps&tricks

Häufig kannst du mit Vorsilben Wörter mit entgegengesetzter Bedeutung bilden, z. B. *happy – unhappy* (glücklich – unglücklich) *possible – impossible* (möglich – unmöglich) *advantage – disadvantage* (Vorteil – Nachteil)

Manchmal gelingt dies auch mit der Nachsilbe -less, z. B. *useful – useless* (nützlich – nutzlos). Auf der folgenden Seite findest du eine Übersicht.

Mit Vorsilben bzw. Nachsilben zu bildende *opposites*.

happy	unhappy	*glücklich*	*unglücklich*
pleasant	unpleasant	*angenehm*	*unangenehm*
reliable	unreliable	*zuverlässig*	*unzuverlässig*
employment	unemployment	*Arbeit*	*Arbeitslosigkeit*
dress	undress	*sich anziehen*	*sich ausziehen*

correct	incorrect	*richtig*	*unrichtig*
complete	incomplete	*vollständig*	*unvollständig*
polite	impolite	*höflich*	*unhöflich*
possible	impossible	*möglich*	*unmöglich*
regular	irregular	*regelmäßig*	*unregelmäßig*

agree	disagree	*übereinstimmen*	*nicht übereinstimmen*
appear	disappear	*erscheinen*	*verschwinden*
like	dislike	*mögen*	*nicht mögen*
agreement	disagreement	*Übereinstimmung*	*Uneinigkeit, Meinungsverschiedenheit*
advantage	disadvantage	*Vorteil*	*Nachteil*
honest	dishonest	*ehrlich*	*unehrlich*
interested	disinterested	*interessiert*	*uninteressiert*

useful	useless	*nützlich*	*nutzlos*

Where did the teddy bear get its name from?

Teddy bear experts think the name goes back to Theodore Roosevelt, President of the United States from 1901 to 1909. In 1902, Roosevelt went on a hunting trip. He happened to find a bear that was tied to a tree with a rope. Some people said later that the bear was only a cub[1].

Roosevelt refused to shoot it because he thought it was not fair and it was not real hunting. All the newspapers printed the story. A newspaper artist drew a picture of Roosevelt and the bear. He did it in a funny way to express a political opinion about the President. Soon the bear became a symbol of Roosevelt and so it was given his nickname "Teddy".

1 cub (Junges)

21 Complete the sentences by using the correct form of the word in brackets.

a) Theodore Roosevelt was a famous (political) . . . .

b) The (popular) . . . . of teddy bears is still increasing.

c) It is not easy to give a psychological (explain) . . . . about people's behaviour.

d) The newspaper artist's (draw) . . . . of Roosevelt became very popular.

e) The President's (refuse) . . . . to shoot the cub was understood by most people.

tipps&tricks

Häufig kannst du Wörter aus einer Wortfamilie von Grundwörtern ableiten. Du solltest dich daher mit den wichtigsten Nachsilben bzw. Endungen vertraut machen, z. B.

*b) popular → popular**ity**,*
*c) explain → explana**tion**,*
*d) draw → draw**ing**,*
e) refuse → refusal.

Achte auf Besonderheiten der Rechtschreibung, wie bei *explain – explanation.*

22 **Complete the sentences with words of the same word family.**

a) Geoff plays **football** every Saturday. He is an excellent . . . .

b) The matches usually **begin** at 3 p.m., but the . . . . may vary.

c) Geoff's team was very . . . . (success) last winter.

d) When they won a match his friends came and. . . . . (congratulation) him.

e) Football hasn't lost its immense . . . . (attract).

tipps&tricks

Das Ausgangswort ist unterstrichen oder in Klammern angegeben. Überlege dir die richtige *Wortart*, z. B. a) ein *Substantiv* (Person), b) ebenfalls ein *Substantiv* (Begriff), c) ein *Adjektiv* und d) ein *Verb* (im *simple past*, wie *they won*).

23 **Who are they?**

Wir suchen Bezeichnungen für Personen.

INFO

a) Bill often plays the **piano**. He wants to be a ... .
b) Jack likes **music** very much. His aim is to be a ... .
c) Mr Brown **builds** houses. He is a ... .
d) Miss Pink **teaches** geography and biology. She is a ... .
e) Miss Black **types** letters in an office. She is a ... .
f) A man **kidnapped** a baby. The ... was caught by the police.
g) The old man is **begging** for money. You can see lots of ... here.
h) Jane **visited** London. She met lots of other ... there.

tipps&tricks

Es gibt einige Endungen bzw. Nachsilben, mit denen du aus einem Grundwort die Bezeichnung für eine Person ableiten kannst, z. B. -ist, -er, -ian, -or, -ar.

24 **Find the nouns of the same word family.**

a) That ... (build) over there is two hundred years old.
b) The pupils are allowed to use their ... (calculate) during the exam.
c) Susan and her father had a ... (discuss) about old times.
d) Do you want to see my new ... (draw)?
e) Jason has a good ... (know) of physics.
f) What is the exact ... (mean) of this sign?

tipps&tricks

Mit den Endungen -ing, -ion, -ation und anderen bildest du Substantive (Sachen und Begriffe).

Find the adjectives.

g) The bus was (crowd) ... .
h) It is (noise) ... in this room.
i) Peter got very (anger) ... .
j) Susan has a (value) ... necklace.
k) John was (luck) ... . He won a (wonder) ... prize.
l) The weather is (change) ... at this time of the year.

tipps&tricks

Adjektive enden oft auf -ful, -ed, -y oder -able.

Find the abstract nouns.

m) to apply
n) to argue
o) to chose
p) to destroy
q) to fail
r) to lose
s) to qualify
t) to recognize
u) to reduce
v) to sell
w) to solve
x) to weigh

tipps&tricks

Du bildest einige sehr schwierige abstrakte Substantive.

Wortbildung mit Nachsilben bzw. Endungen.

Grundwort		abgeleitete Wörter		
listen	**-er**	listener	*Zuhörer*	
act	**-or**	actor	*Schauspieler*	**Personen**
cycle	**-ist**	cyclist	*Radfahrer*	
cook	**-er**	cooker	*Herd*	**Sachen**
arrive	**-al**	arrival	*Ankunft*	
appear	**-ance**	appearance	*Erscheinung*	
examine	**-ation**	examination	*Prüfung*	
differ	**-ence**	difference	*Unterschied*	
cross	**-ing**	crossing	*Überfahrt*	**abstrakte**
define	**-ition**	definition	*Definition*	**Substantive**
elect	**-ion**	election	*Wahl*	aus
decide	**-sion**	decision	*Entscheidung*	Verben
complain	**-t**	complaint	*Beschwerde*	oder
grow	**-th**	growth	*Wachstum*	Adjektiven
fail	**-ure**	failure	*Misserfolg*	
active	**-ity**	activity	*Aktivität*	
happy	**-ness**	happiness	*Glück*	
true	**-th**	truth	*Wahrheit*	
difficult	**-y**	difficulty	*Schwierigkeit*	
accept	**-able**	acceptable	*annehmbar*	
please	**-ant**	pleasant	*angenehm*	
differ	**-ent**	different	*unterschiedlich*	
fashion	**-able**	fashionable	*modisch*	**Adjektive**
person	**-al**	personal	*persönlich*	aus
wood	**-en**	wooden	*hölzern*	Verben
care	**-ful**	careful	*sorgsam*	oder
atom	**-ic**	atomic	*atomar*	Substantiven
care	**-less**	careless	*sorglos*	
danger	**-ous**	dangerous	*gefährlich*	
cloud	**-y**	cloudy	*bewölkt*	

tipps&tricks

Nach diesem Muster kannst du zahlreiche neue Wörter ableiten.

INFO Versuche die Aufgaben mithilfe der kopierten Seiten aus einem Lexikon (→ S. 51/53) zu lösen.

25 Complete the following sentences.

Du warst eingeladen und erzählst später einem Freund/einer Freundin in einem Brief einiges über deine Unterhaltung mit den Gästen. Die unterstrichenen Wörter fehlen dir. Du schlägst sie im Wörterbuch nach.

Du hast unter anderem gesagt, dass

a) du dich freust, ihn <u>kennen zu lernen.</u>
b) du sie schon seit vielen Jahren <u>kennst.</u>
c) du <u>kein Mitleid kennst</u>, wenn jemand zu viel raucht.
d) es interessant sei, jemanden <u>von einer bestimmten Seite kennen zu lernen</u>.
e) dieses Problem sich <u>deiner Kenntnis entzieht.</u>
f) du ein großer <u>Kenner</u> von Gemälden bist.

a) I'm pleased .... him.

b) I have .... her for many years.

c) I .... if someone smokes too much.

d) It is interesting .... of somebody.

e) I .... of that problem.

f) I'm a great .... of paintings.

löffel) ladle; **b)** *(Signalstab)* signalling disc; **c)** *(Maurer~)* trowel
Keller ['kɛlɐ] **der; ~s, ~ a)** cellar; *(~geschoß)* basement; **der Dol-lar[kurs] ist in den ~ gegangen** *(fig.)* the dollar has gone through the floor *(fig.)*; **im ~ sein** *(Skat Jargon)* have a minus score *or* minus points; **b)** *(Luftschutz~)* [air-raid] shelter; **c)** *s.* **Kellerlokal**
Keller·assel die wood-louse
Kellerei die; ~, ~en winery; wine producer's
Keller-: ~fenster das cellar window; *(von ~geschoß)* basement window; **~geschoß das** basement; **~gewölbe das** underground vault; **~lokal das** cellar bar/disco/restaurant *etc.*; **~treppe die** cellar stairs *pl.*; **~wohnung die** basement flat *(Brit.) or (Amer.)* apartment
Kellner ['kɛlnɐ] **der; ~s, ~:** waiter
Kellnerin die; ~, ~nen waitress
kellnern *itr. V. (ugs.)* work as a waiter/waitress
Kelte ['kɛltə] **der; ~n, ~n** Celt
Kelter ['kɛltɐ] **die; ~, ~n** fruit-press; *(für Trauben)* winepress
keltern *tr. V.* press *(grapes etc.)*
keltisch *Adj.* Celtic
Keltisch das; ~[s] Celtic
Kenia ['ke:nia] **(das); ~s** Kenya
Kenianer [ke'nia:nɐ] **der; ~s, ~, Kenianerin die; ~, ~nen** Kenyan
kennen ['kɛnən] *unr. tr. V.* **a)** know; **das Leben ~:** know about life; know the ways of the world; **das ~ wir gar nicht anders** it's always been like that; **kennst du ihn?** do you know who he is?; *(bist du mit ihm bekannt)* are you acquainted with him?; **kennst du den?** *(diesen Witz)* have you heard this one?; **jmds. Bücher/Werk ~:** know *or* be acquainted with sb.'s books/work; **da kennst du mich aber schlecht** *(ugs.)* that just shows you don't know me very well; **das kennen wir [schon]** *(ugs. abwertend)* we've heard all that before; **sich nicht mehr ~ [vor ...]** be beside oneself [with ...]; **da kenne ich/da kennt er nichts** *(ugs.)* and to hell with everything else *(coll.)*; **b)** *(bekannt sein mit)* know; be acquainted with; **jmdn. flüchtig/persönlich ~:** know sb. slightly/personally; **die beiden ~ sich nicht mehr** *(fig.)* the two are no longer on speaking terms; **ich glaube, wir beide ~ uns noch nicht** I don't think we've been introduced; **c)** *(haben)* have; **keinen Winter/Sommer ~:** have no winter/summer; **er kennt keine Kopfschmerzen** he never gets a headache; **kein Mitleid ~:** know *or* have no pity; **d)** *(wiedererkennen)* know; recognize; **na, kennst du mich noch?** well, do you remember me?
kennen|lernen *tr. V.* get to know; **jmdn./etw. [näher] ~:** get to know sb./sth. [better]; become [better] acquainted with sb./sth.; **jmdn. ~** *(jmdm. erstmals begegnen)* meet sb.; **jmdn. von einer bestimmten Seite ~:** see a particular side of sb.; **jmdn. als einen bescheidenen Menschen** *usw.* **~:** come to know sb. as a modest person *etc.*; **du wirst mich noch ~!** you'll find out I don't stand for any nonsense; **[es] freut mich, Sie kennenzulernen** pleased to meet you; pleased to make your acquaintance *(formal)*
Kenner der; ~s, ~ a) expert, authority (+ *Gen.* on); **b)** *(von Wein, Speisen)* connoisseur
Kennerblick der expert eye; **mit ~:** with an expert eye
Kenn-: ~karte die identity card; **~marke die** [police] identification badge; ≈ [police] warrant card *or (Amer.)* ID card; **~melodie die** *(Rundf.)* signature tune; **~nummer die** *s.* **Kennummer**
kenntlich ['kɛntlɪç] *Adj.* **in ~ sein** be recognizable *or* distinguishable **(an** by); **jmdn./etw. ~ machen** mark sth./make sb. [easily] identifiable; **etw. als Gift ~ machen** mark *or* label sth. as a poison
Kenntnis ['kɛntnɪs] **die; ~, ~se a)** *o. Pl.* knowledge; **von etw. ~ haben/erhalten** be informed on sth. *or* have knowledge of sth./learn *or* hear about sth.; **das entzieht sich meiner ~** *(geh.)* I have no knowledge of that; **von etw. ~ nehmen, etw. zur ~ nehmen** take note of sth.; **jmdn. von etw. in ~ setzen** inform *or* notify sb. of sth.; **jmdn. zur ~ nehmen** take notice of sb.; **b)** *Pl.* knowledge *sing.*; **oberflächliche/gründliche ~se in etw.** *(Dat.)* **haben** have a superficial/thorough knowledge of sth.
Kenntnisnahme die; ~ *(Papierdt.)* **jmdm. etw. zur ~ vorlegen** submit sth. to sb. for his/her attention; **nach ~ der Akten** after giving the documents my/his *etc.* attention
kenntnis·reich *Adj.* well-informed; knowledgeable
Kennummer die; ~, ~n reference number; code number
kenn-, Kenn-: ~wort das; *Pl.* **~wörter a)** *(Erkennungszeichen)* code-word; reference; **b)** *(Parole)* password; code-word; **~zahl die a)** *s.* **~ziffer; b)** *(Fernspr.)* code; **~zeichen das a)** *(Merkmal)* sign; mark; **ein ~zeichen eines Genies** a [hall]mark of a genius; **besondere ~zeichen** distinguishing marks; **b)** *(Erkennungszeichen)* badge; *(auf einem Behälter, einer Ware usw.)* label; **c)** *(Kfz-W.)* registration number; **~zeichnen** *tr. V.* **a)** mark; label *(container, goods, etc.)*; mark, signpost *(way)*; tag *(bird, animal)*; **etw. als ... ~zeichnen** mark *or* identify sth. as ...; **b)** *(charakterisieren)* characterize; **jmdn. als ... ~zeichnen** characterize sb. as ...; **c)** *(in seiner Eigenart erkennen lassen)* typify; **jmdn. als ... ~zeichnen** mark sb. out as ...; **~zeichnend** *Adj.* typical, characteristic **(für** of); **~zeichnung die a)** marking; *(von Behältern, Waren)* labelling; *(von Vögeln, Tieren)* tagging; **b)** *(Charakterisierung)* characterization; **c)** *(Kennzeichen)* mark; **~ziffer die** reference number; *(bei einem Zeitungsinserat)* box number
kentern ['kɛntɐn] *itr. V.; mit sein* capsize
Keramik [ke'ra:mɪk] **die; ~, ~en a)** *o. Pl. (gebrannter Ton)* ceramics *pl.*; pottery; **b)** *(~gegenstand)* ceramic; piece of pottery; **c)** *(Material)* fired clay; **d)** *o. Pl. (Technik)* ceramics *sing.*; pottery
keramisch *Adj.; nicht präd.* ceramic
Kerbe ['kɛrbə] **die; ~, ~n** notch; **in dieselbe** *od.* **die gleiche ~ hauen** *(ugs.)* take the same line
Kerbel ['kɛrbl̩] **der; ~s** chervil
kerben *tr. V.* notch; **etw. in etw.** *(Akk.)* **~:** carve sth. into sth.
Kerb-: ~holz das *in* **etwas/einiges auf dem ~holz haben** *(ugs.)* have done a job/a job or two *(sl.)*; **~tier das** insect
Kerker ['kɛrkɐ] **der; ~s, ~ a)** *(hist.) (Gefängnis)* dungeons *pl.*; *(Zelle)* dungeon; **b)** *(österr., hist.; Strafe)* imprisonment
Kerl [kɛrl] **der; ~s, ~e** *(nordd., md. auch:* **~s) a)** *(ugs.; männliche Person)* fellow *(coll.)*; chap *(coll.)*; bloke *(Brit. sl.)*; **ein ganzer** *od.* **richtiger ~:** a splendid fellow *(coll.) or* chap *(coll.)*; **ein gemeiner/frecher ~** *(abwertend)* a nasty so-and-so *(coll.)*/an impudent fellow *(coll.)*; **b)** *(ugs.; sympathischer Mensch)* **er ist ein feiner ~:** he's a fine chap *(coll.) or (sl.)* a good bloke; **sie ist ein netter/feiner ~:** she's a nice/fine woman

(Duden Oxford Standardwörterbuch Englisch)

26 **Translate the words and expressions in bold print in the following sentences into German.**

a) In his **spare time** Mr Ward likes to read books about the **space age.**

b) He watched a film where a **spaceship** was sent into **space** and one of the **spacemen** made a **space walk.**

c) At the cinema there was one **spare** seat.

d) When he drove home, he realised that one tyre of his car had a puncture but he had left the **spare wheel** in the garage.

e) So he asked his friend if he could put him up in their **spare room.**

f) They arrived at his friend's house in **the space of an hour.**

27 **Choose suitable definitions for the words in bold print and write down the German meaning.**

a) Mr Ward lives in a beautiful countryside. He loves the **wide open spaces.**

b) There are vast green areas around the town – a lot of **spacious** parks.

c) Mr Ward has got a friend who comes from Spain. He is **Spanish.**

d) He knows that his friend is a clever person. He often says: **He is a bright spark.**

South Pole 570

land *pr. n.* Südengland *(das); attrib.* südenglisch; ~ **'Pole** *pr. n.* Südpol, *der;* ~ **'Seas** *pr. n. pl.* Südsee, *die*

southward ['saʊθwəd] **1.** *adj.* nach Süden gerichtet; *(situated towards the south)* südlich; **in a ~ direction** nach Süden; [in] Richtung Süden. **2.** *adv.* südwärts; **they are ~ bound** sie fahren nach *od.* [in] Richtung Süden

southwards ['saʊθwədz] *adv.* südwärts

south: ~-**'west 1.** *n.* Südwesten, *der;* **2.** *adj.* südwestlich; Südwest⟨*wind, -küste*⟩; **3.** *adv.* südwestwärts; nach Südwesten; **S~-West 'Africa** *pr. n.* Südwestafrika, *(das);* ~-**'western** *adj.* südwestlich

souvenir [su:və'nɪə(r)] *n. (of holiday)* Andenken, *das;* Souvenir, *das* (**of** aus); *(of wedding-day, one's youth, etc.)* Andenken, *das* (**of** an + *Akk.*)

sou'wester [saʊ'westə(r)] *n.* **a)** *(hat)* Südwester, *der;* **b)** *(coat)* Ölhaut, *die*

sovereign ['sɒvrɪn] *n.* **a)** *(ruler)* Souverän, *der;* **b)** *(Brit. Hist.: coin)* Sovereign, *der;* 20-Shilling-Münze, *die*

sovereignty ['sɒvrɪntɪ] *n.* Souveränität, *die;* Oberhoheit, *die*

Soviet ['səʊvɪət, 'sɒvɪət] **1.** *adj.* sowjetisch; Sowjet⟨*bürger, -literatur, -kultur, -ideologie*⟩. **2.** *n.* Sowjet, *der*

Soviet 'Union *pr. n.* Sowjetunion, *die*

¹sow [səʊ] *v. t., p.p.* **sown** [səʊn] *or* **~ed** [səʊd] **a)** *(plant)* [aus]säen; **b)** *(plant with seed)* einsäen, besäen ⟨*Feld, Boden*⟩; **c)** *(cover thickly)* spicken *(ugs.)*

²sow [saʊ] *n. (female pig)* Sau, *die*

sown *see* ¹sow

soya [bean] ['sɔɪə (bi:n)], **soy bean** ['sɔɪ bi:n] *ns.* **a)** *(plant)* Soja[bohne], *die;* **b)** *(seed)* Sojabohne, *die*

soy sauce ['sɔɪ sɔ:s] *n.* Sojasoße, *die*

sozzled ['sɒzld] *adj. (sl.)* voll *(ugs.)*

spa [spɑ:] *n.* **a)** *(place)* Bad, *das;* Badeort, *der;* **b)** *(spring)* Mineralquelle, *die*

space [speɪs] **1.** *n.* **a)** Raum, *der;* **stare into ~:** in die Luft *od.* ins Leere starren; **b)** *(interval between points)* Platz, *der;* **clear a ~:** Platz schaffen; **c)** *(area on page)* Platz, *der;* **d) the wide open ~s** das weite, flache Land; **e)** *(Astron.)* Weltraum, *der; see also* **outer space; f)** *(blank between words)* Zwischenraum, *der;* **g)** *(interval of time)* Zeitraum, *der;* **in the ~ of a minute/an hour** *etc.* innerhalb einer Minute/Stunde *usw.* **2.** *v. t.* **the posts are ~d at intervals of one metre** die Pfosten sind im Abstand von einem Meter aufgestellt

~ **'out** *v. t.* verteilen

space: ~ **age** *n.* [Welt]raumzeitalter, *das;* Zeitalter der Raumfahrt, *das;* **~-bar** *n.* Leertaste, *die;* **~craft** *n.* Raumfahrzeug, *das; (unmanned)* Raumsonde, *die;* ~ **flight** *n.* **a)** *(a journey through ~)* [Welt]raumflug, *der;* **b)** *see* ~ **travel; ~-heater** *n.* Heizgerät, *das;* **~man** *n.* Raumfahrer, *der*/-fahrerin, *die;* **~-saving** *adj.* platzsparend; **~ship** *n.* Raumschiff, *das;* ~ **shuttle** *n.* Raumfähre, *die;* Raumtransporter, *der;* ~ **station** *n.* [Welt]raumstation, *die;* **~suit** *n.* Raumanzug, *der;* ~ **travel** *n.* Raumfahrt, *die;* ~ **walk** *n.* Spaziergang im All

spacing ['speɪsɪŋ] *n.* Zwischenraum, *der; (Printing)* Sperrungen; Spationierung, *die (Druckw.);* **single/double** ~ *(on typewriter)* einfacher/doppelter Zeilenabstand

spacious ['speɪʃəs] *adj.* **a)** *(vast in area)* weitläufig ⟨*Garten, Park, Ländereien*⟩; **b)** *(roomy)* geräumig ⟨*Raum*⟩; breit ⟨*Straße*⟩

spade [speɪd] *n.* **a)** Spaten, *der;* **call a ~ a ~:** das Kind beim [rechten] Namen nennen *(ugs.);* **b)** *(Cards)* Pik, *das; see also* **club 1 d**

'spadework *n. (preliminary work)* Vorarbeit, *die*

spaghetti [spə'getɪ] *n.* Spaghetti *Pl.*

Spain [speɪn] *pr. n.* Spanien *(das)*

Spam, (P) [spæm] *n.* Frühstücksfleisch, *das*

¹span [spæn] **1.** *n.* **a)** *(full extent)* Spanne, *die;* ~ **of life/time** Lebens-/Zeitspanne, *die;* **b)** *(of bridge)* Spannweite, *die.* **2.** *v. t.,* **-nn-** überspannen ⟨*Fluß*⟩; umfassen ⟨*Zeitraum*⟩

²span *see* **spick**

spangle ['spæŋgl] **1.** *n. see* **sequin. 2.** *v. t.* **~d with stars/buttercups** von glitzernden Sternen/mit leuchtenden Butterblumen übersät

Spaniard ['spænjəd] *n.* Spanier, *der*/Spanierin, *die*

spaniel ['spænjəl] *n.* Spaniel, *der*

Spanish ['spænɪʃ] **1.** *adj.* spanisch; **sb. is ~:** jmd. ist Spanier/Spanierin. **2.** *n.* **a)** *(language)* Spanisch, *das; see also* **English 2 a; b)** *constr. as pl. (people)* Spanier

spank [spæŋk] **1.** *n.* ≈ Klaps, *der (ugs.).* **2.** *v. t.* ~ **sb.** jmdm. den Hintern versohlen *(ugs.);* **get ~ed** den Hintern voll kriegen *(ugs.)*

spanking ['spæŋkɪŋ] *n.* Tracht Prügel, *die (ugs.)*

spanner ['spænə(r)] *n. (Brit.)* Schraubenschlüssel, *der;* **put** *or* **throw a ~ in the works** *(fig.)* Sand ins Getriebe streuen

¹spar [spɑ:(r)] *v. i.,* **-rr-** *(Boxing)* sparren

²spar *n. (pole)* Rundholz, *das;* Spiere, *die (Seemannsspr.)*

spare [speə(r)] **1.** *adj.* **a)** *(not in use)* übrig; ~ **time/moment** Freizeit, *die*/freier Augenblick; **there is one ~ seat** ein Platz ist noch frei; **are there any ~ tickets for Friday?** gibt es noch Karten für Freitag?; **b)** *(for use when needed)* zusätzlich, Extra⟨*bett, -tasse*⟩; ~ **room** Gästezimmer, *das;* **go ~** *(Brit. sl.: be very angry)* durchdrehen *(salopp).* **2.** *n.* Ersatzteil, *das*/-reifen, *der usw.* **3.** *v. t.* **a)** *(do without)* entbehren; **can you ~ me a moment?** hast du einen Augenblick Zeit für mich?; **we arrived with ten minutes to ~:** wir kamen zehn Minuten früher an; **b)** *(not inflict on)* ~ **sb. sth.** jmdm. etw. ersparen; **c)** *(not hurt)* [ver]schonen; **d)** *(fail to use)* **not ~ any expense/pains** *or* **efforts** keine Kosten/Mühe scheuen; **no expense ~d** an nichts gespart. *See also* **rod c**

spare: ~ **'part** *n.* Ersatzteil, *das;* ~ **'tyre** *n.* **a)** Reserve-, Ersatzreifen, *der;* **b)** *(Brit. fig. coll.)* Rettungsring, *der (ugs.);* ~ **'wheel** *n.* Ersatzrad, *das*

sparing ['speərɪŋ] *adj.* sparsam; **be ~ of sth./in the use of sth.** mit etw. sparsam umgehen

spark [spɑ:k] **1.** *n.* **a)** Funke, *der;* **the ~s [begin to] fly** *(fig.)* es funkt *(ugs.);* **a ~ of generosity/decency** *(fig.)* ein Funke[n] Großzügigkeit/Anstand; **b)** *(in sparking-plug)* Zündfunke[n], *der (Kfz-W.);* **c) a bright ~** *(clever person; also iron.)* ein schlauer Kopf. **2.** *v. t. see* ~ **off**

~ **'off** *v. t.* **a)** *(cause to explode)* zünden; **b)** *(fig.: start)* auslösen

'sparking-plug *n. (Brit. Motor Veh.)* Zündkerze, *die*

sparkle ['spɑ:kl] **1.** *v. i.* **a)** *(flash)* ⟨*Tautropfen:*⟩ glitzern; ⟨*Augen:*⟩ funkeln, sprühen; **b)** *(perform brilliantly)* glänzen; **c)** *(be lively)* sprühen (**with** vor + *Dat.*). **2.** *n.* Glitzern, *das;* Funkeln, *das*

(Duden Oxford Standardwörterbuch Englisch)

3. Grammar

INFO

Du sollst einen Lückentext mit vermischten Aufgaben zur Grammatik *(mixed grammar)* bearbeiten. Du musst die Wörter in Klammern in der richtigen Form einsetzen oder – falls dies notwendig ist *(if necessary)* – selber ein Wort/mehrere Wörter finden.

1 Complete the text using the words in brackets in their right form and add words where necessary.

a) Yesterday Mike, a student of music from London, (listen)

. . . . to several buskers in Munich's pedestrian zone.

tipps&tricks

Yesterday hilft dir, die richtige Zeit des Verbs *listen* zu finden – *simple past* oder *past progressive.*

b) He was delighted to meet musicians . . . . so many different countries.

tipps&tricks

musicians ... *(aus)* ...

c) Manuel, a (Spain) . . . . guitarist,

(just/finish) . . . . when Mike arrived.

tipps&tricks

Bilde das Adjektiv von *Spain* und denke an den großen Anfangsbuchstaben bei Ableitungen von Ländern, *when Mike arrived (simple past)* bedingt die Vorvergangenheit *(past perfect)* von *finish* mit eingeschobenem *just* oder die Verlaufsform des *past (past progressive).*

d) He (turn) . . . . to an (Austria) . . . . girl, who (play) . . . . the accordeon.

tipps&tricks

Bilde das Adjektiv von *Austria* und beachte den großen Anfangsbuchstaben.
Für das Verb *turn* gilt weiter das Signal *yesterday*, ebenso wie bei *play*, wobei hier das *past progressive* sinnvoll wäre (sie spielte gerade!).

e) Mike had never heard anyone play this instrument (good) . . . . than her.

tipps&tricks

than verweist auf die Steigerungsform (Komparativ) von *good* (besser als).

f) She told him that she (be) . . . . unemployed and (need/make) . . . . some money.

tipps&tricks

Weiter im *simple past: Yesterday* und auch she *told*; she needed + *to* make

g) She went on to say that she really (enjoy/make) . . . . music even if she (not/like) . . . . having to earn her living this way.

tipps&tricks

Weiter *simple past* von *enjoy* und der verneinten Form von *like* (did); nach *enjoy* folgt die -ing-Form.

h) Some buskers from Peru (dress) .... in

(beauty) .... national costumes, were

playing (extreme/good)...

tipps&tricks

Verkürzter Relativsatz mit *dress* in passiver Form (die gekleidet waren); Adjektiv von *beauty*; beide Male Adverb von *good (They were playing)* und *extreme* (Wie gut?).

i) Besides they seemed to be enjoying (oneself) .... a lot.

tipps&tricks

Richtige Form von *oneself* zu *they* ...

j) If it (start/rain/not)..,

Mike could have listened to their music for hours on end.

tipps&tricks

Richtige Zeitkombination für den if-Satz: Zu *could have listened* im Hauptsatz gehört *past perfect* im if-Satz: if-Satz Typ 3

2 **Fill in the correct forms of the words in brackets. Add prepositions where necessary.**

Traffic on 21st Century Roads

a) Nowadays Britain (to suffer) . . . . the "car disease" according to a Greenpeace report. It says that the road traffic in Britain (to grow) . . . . by 57 percent in the past 10 years.

b) The number of car owners (to expect) . . . . to rise from 19 million to 35 million by the year 2025 with the government plans (to build) . . . . many more new roads.

c) The report warns that if we do not stop (to poison) . . . . the environment with exhaust fumes the climate (to change) . . . . (drastic/drastically).

d) Moreover, five thousand people (to die) . . . . in road accidents each year.

e) The fact that some years ago the number of car accidents was much (low) . . . . suggests that the interests of cyclists and pedestrians, pensioners and children (to ignore) . . . . too long.

f) The report also points to methods (to control) . . . . car use in Europe and America.

g) Greenpeace concludes that banning cars from city centres would be the (efficient) . . . . way of fighting smog from cars and increasing road safety.

3 **Fill in the correct forms of the words in brackets.**

a) Thirty years ago 28 % of American women (to work) .... outside their homes. Nowadays 68 % have a job. Susan Smith from the University of Florida says: "The trends for the coming year are very (clear/clearly) .... Moms will keep (to work) ...."

b) In Great Britain there is a similar development. The number of women who want both to have children and have a career (to increase) .... in the last ten years. Most couples where both partners work believe in (to share) .... housework and child care. But a recent survey showed that in 1990 it was mostly women who (must) .... look after their children. Although fathers (to spend) .... more time with their children now, they (still, not, share) .... the daily household chores like (cook) .... meals. For many years people (say) .... that children would be better off if mothers (stay) .... at home. This is (probable/probably) .... not completely right. Mothers get satisfaction from their careers and this benefits the children too. The problem of whether to have a career or not (must, solve) .... by the woman herself. In the future it seems certain that more women (decide) .... to combine work and having a job.

4 **Fill in the words in brackets in the correct form. You may have to add words.**

iNFO

Du sollst die in Klammern angeführten Wörter in der richtigen Form einsetzen bzw. selber ein Wort/Wörter finden, das/die sinngemäß in die Lücke passt/passen *(You may have to add words).*

An old lady.

a) An old lady, ... was making her very first . . . . (fly) in an airliner, was very (nervous) . . . . and insisted . . . . speaking to the captain . . . . take-off.

b) "You will bring me down safely, ... ?" she asked (anxious) . . . .

c) "Don't worry, madam," replied the captain cheerfully. I've never left . . . . up there yet."

A good lady.

d) A hungry-looking tramp knocked . . . . the kitchen door and asked . . . . . . something to eat. The woman of the house . . . . felt a bit (uneasy) . . . . , replied, "If I give you a piece of my home-made apple-pie, will you promise to go away and not come back?"

e) "Well, you know your cooking better . . . . I do, lady," said the tramp.

tipps&tricks

Es kann sein, dass kein Wort in die Satzlücke gehört (You *may* have to add – *Es kann sein,* dass du hinzufügen musst ...). Setze also einen Querstrich in diese Lücke, damit klar wird, dass du die Aufgabe nicht übersehen hast.

5 Complete the sentences. Add the missing words where necessary.

INFO Finde geeignete Wörter für die Lücken oder mache einen Strich —.

a) May I introduce . . . . ? My name is Tom.

I like hobbies, ... collecting stamps or playing cards.

I like neither football . . . . hockey.

b) The girl . . . . you see over there is my sister.

I wonder . . . . where she bought the new T-shirt.

The old . . . . was so dirty that she threw it away.

c) Sue can't speak French, and I can't . . . .

She goes to school . . . . foot; she doesn't go . . . . bus.

d) Lessons begin . . . . 8 o'clock . . . . Monday.

The pupils can choose . . . . several subjects.

e) I can't remember . . . . where I have left my umbrella.

You will help me to find it, ... ? – Of course, I . . . .

Survival Kit

Lückentexte bearbeiten – Möglichkeiten und Tipps

a) Bestätigungsfragen oder Kurzantwort: You will come, *won't you*? – Yes, *I will*.

b) Relativpronomen: *who, which, that, whose*

c) Teile eines Vergleichs: *as* ... *as*, better *than*

d) Verbindungen wie: *either* ... *or* (entweder ... oder), *neither* ... *nor* (weder ... noch)

e) Die Pronomen *one* (für ein nicht mehr genanntes Wort im Singular) bzw. *ones* (Plural): a blue cap and a red *one*

f) Das *self-Pronomen* in der zutreffenden Form: *She* enjoyed *herself, he* did it *himself* oder *each other/one another:* They write to *each other* twice a week. oder nichts: to move (**sich** bewegen), to remember (**sich** erinnern **an**)

g) Eine Präposition: *in, on, at, around, ...*
oder eine Konjunktion: *although, because, but, ...*

6 **Use the verbs in brackets in the correct form.**

Es folgen Übungen, die eine gute Vorbereitung auf vermischte Grammatikaufgaben sind, weil einzelne Aspekte zunächst isoliert geübt werden. Bilde die richtige **Zeitform** der in Klammern angegebenen **Verben**.

INFO

a) What .... Susan .... (do) just now?

She .... (watch) the quizz show on TV.

She .... (watch) it every afternoon at three o'clock.

b) Why .... Jason .... (miss) the football training yesterday?

He .... (fall off) a tree and ....

(break) his arm two days ago and .... (have to) stay at home.

c) Our town .... (change) a lot in the last few years.

Some blocks of flats .... (build); unfortunately

the by-pass................................... (not, finish) yet.

d) Susan is so happy; she .... (just, pass) her driving test.

She.................. (be) eighteen next week and she hopes her parents

.... (allow) her to take the family car for a drive.

tipps&tricks

Achte auf den Sinnzusammenhang des Satzes/der Sätze und auf mögliche Signalwörter, um die richtige Zeit (z. B. *present, past, present perfect*) bzw. Form *(active or passive)* zu finden, z. B. a) *just now* verweist auf *present progressive*, b) *yesterday* auf *past tense*, c) *in the last few years* sagt dir, dass du *present perfect* bilden musst, wobei du noch zwischen *active* und *passive* unterscheiden musst.

7 **Mind the tenses – active or passive?**

> Überlege dir die richtige Zeitform, indem du dir den Sinn der Sätze klarmachst und Signalwörter beachtest. Überlege auch, ob du die aktive (jemand macht etwas) oder die passive Form (etwas wird gemacht, jemand erleidet etwas) bilden musst.
>
> INFO

a) The old bridge .... (must, repair).

We hope it .... (repair) soon.

b) How long .... you .... (learn) English now?

I .... (learn) it for six years.

c) When .... you .... (travel) to England?

I think it .... (be) two years ago.

d) How old .... (be) Jill?

She .... (be) sixteen, but she .... (be) seventeen next week.

e) There .... (be) an accident in the High Street yesterday.

Two pedestrians .... (injure) and .... (must, take) to hospital.

f) .... you ever .... (be) to Ireland?

I'm afraid, I ....

But I .... (already, make) plans.

I .... (fly) to Dublin with my sister in August.

g) What .... you .... (do) at ten o'clock last night?

I .... (watch) the football match on TV.

Our team.................. (score) twice and .... (win) easily.

JOKE

"Last winter during the dark nights I dressed all in white so that the traffic would see me."
"Did that keep you safe?"
"No. I was knocked down by a snow-plough[1]."

1 (Schneepflug)

Die Zeiten im Aktiv

Tenses	simple	Signalwörter	progressive	Signalwörter
Present	I ask *Ich frage*	always, sometimes, often, never, every ...	I am asking *Ich frage (gerade)*	just now, at the moment
Past	I asked *Ich fragte*	yesterday, last ... in 1990, ... ago, When?	I was asking *Ich fragte (gerade)*	yesterday at ... o'clock ... when I came
Present Perfect	I have asked *Ich habe gefragt*	since, not ... yet for (now)	I have been asking *Ich habe (gerade) gefragt*	
Past Perfect	I had asked *Ich hatte gefragt*		I had been asking *Ich hatte (gerade) gefragt*	
Future	I will ask *Ich werde fragen*	tomorrow, next ... *if-Satz Typ 1*	I will be asking *Ich werde (gerade) fragen*	
Future Perfect	I will have asked *Ich werde gefragt haben*	*if-Satz Typ 1*	I will have been asking *Ich werde (gerade) gefragt haben*	
Conditional	I would ask *Ich würde fragen*	*if-Satz Typ 2*	I would be asking *Ich würde (gerade) fragen*	
Conditional Perfect	I would have asked *Ich würde gefragt haben*	*if-Satz Typ 3*	I would have been asking *Ich würde (gerade) gefragt haben*	
Bildung			to be + ing	

Die Zeiten im Passiv

Tenses	simple	Signalwörter	progressive
Present	I am asked *Ich werde gefragt*	always, sometimes, often, never, every ...	I am being asked *Ich werde gerade gefragt*
Past	I was asked *Ich wurde gefragt*	yesterday, last ... in 1990, ... ago, When?	I was being asked *Ich wurde gerade gefragt*
Present Perfect	I have been asked *Ich bin gefragt worden*	since, not ... yet for (now)	
Past Perfect	I had been asked *Ich war gefragt worden*		
Future	I will be asked *Ich werde gefragt werden*	tomorrow, next ...	
Future Perfect	I will have been asked *Ich werde gefragt worden sein*		
Conditional	I would be asked *Ich würde gefragt werden*		
Conditional Perfect	I would have been asked *Ich würde gefragt worden sein*		
Bildung	to be + Partizip Perfekt		to be + being + Partizip Perfekt

8 Put the verbs in brackets into the correct form.

INFO Du sollst die Verben in dem Satzteil mit *if* bzw. im Hauptsatz in die richtige Zeitform setzen.

a) If it rains this afternoon, we . . . . (stay) at home.
We . . . . (not, can, go) swimming in the lake.
What a pity!

b) If I won a lot of money in the pools, I . . . . (travel) around the world. I . . . . (can, see) wonderful places and I . . . . (may, meet) lots of interesting people.

c) If I had missed my bus this morning, I . . . . (walk) to school. I . . . . (may, be) late for the first lesson. No problem!

JOKE
"If you found a pound note, would you keep it?"
"No, vicar."
"That's good boy. What would you do with it?"
"I'd spend it."

tipps&tricks
Erinnere dich an die **3 Typen von if-Sätzen** und beachte die entsprechenden Zeitenkombinationen, z. B. a) In dem Satzteil nach *if* steht das *present*, im Hauptsatz steht *will* (oder ein anderes Modalverb, wie *can* oder *may*) + *infinitive*.
Informiere dich in der Übersicht auf der nächsten Seite!

9 Some more if-clauses.

Überlege anhand der vorliegenden Teile, welcher der drei Typen zutrifft, und bilde die dazugehörige richtige Zeitform.

INFO

a) I .... (buy) the mountain bike if I could afford it.

b) I would stay at home if I .... (be) you.

c) We would have played cricket yesterday if it .... (not, rain) heavily.

d) We'll be late for school if our bus .... (not, come) soon.

e) If you .... (not, phone), your mother will be upset.

f) We.............. (lose) the soccer match if our opponents had played better.

g) The plants will grow if you .... (water) them regularly.

h) If things .... (not, improve), Patrick will lose his job.

i) It .... (be) an advantage if we arrived before seven o'clock.

j) I .... (wear) my coat if it had rained.

if-clauses (Bedingungssätze) Grundmuster

Typ	Satzteil mit if	Hauptsatz
1	**present tense** (z. B. are, asks, come) *Erfüllbare Bedingung*	**will – future** (z. B. will be, won't come) statt will: can, may, must, needn't (z. B. can be, must have) **Imperativ** (z. B. tell ...) *Folge für die Zukunft*
2	**past tense** (z. B. was asked, came) *Nicht oder höchstwahrscheinlich nicht erfüllbare Bedingung*	**conditional** (z. B. would ask) statt would: could, might (z. B. could come, might see) *nur gedachte Folge für die Gegenwart oder Zukunft*
3	**past perfect** (z. B. had been, had asked) *Nicht mehr erfüllbare Bedingung*	**conditional perfect** (z. B. would have been) statt would have: could/might have been *nur gedachte Folge für die Vergangenheit*

10 Complete the sentences using the words in brackets in the correct form.

Susan: Where did you go last night?

Jill: We went to the Odeon cinema. We wanted .... (see) "Die Hard With a Vengeance".

Susan: I saw it last Sunday. I'm fond .... (go) to the pictures. There were lots of people and we had difficulty .... (get) tickets.

Jill: Oh yes. The same happened to me. But we didn't mind .... (queue) at the ticket office for twenty minutes.

tipps&tricks

Du musst entscheiden, ob die in Klammern angegebenen Verben im to-Infinitiv *(to do)* oder in der -ing-Form *(doing)* stehen. Dies hängt von den Wörtern ab, die vorausgehen: Nach *want* folgt z. B. *to-Infinitiv*, nach *fond* schreibst du *of* + *-ing*-Form, nach *difficulty* folgt ebenfalls die *-ing*-Form.

Du kannst die wichtigsten Wörter, nach denen die -ing-Form (auch Wörter + Präpositionen) bzw. der to-Infinitiv folgt, auf der Seite 68 nachschlagen.

JOKE

"Doctor! Doctor! I keep seeing double!"
"Sit on the couch, please."
"Which one?"

11 -ing-form or to-infinitive?

tipps&tricks

Entscheide zwischen den beiden Formen. Bei der -ing-Form solltest du überlegen, ob du zusätzlich eine Präposition finden musst, z. B. bei b) *apologize + ... + -ing-Form*.

a) Tom decided .... (attend) the club meeting.

He dislikes .... (sit) at home in the evening.

b) Susan apologized .... (be) late.

She wanted .... (come) at eight o'clock, but she missed her bus.

c) Peter is looking forward .... (travel) to France next month.

He hopes .... (see) lots of interesting places.

d) Bill says: "It's no use .... (get) up so early."

He is fond .... (sleep) till eleven on Sundays.

e) Andy succeeded .... (pass) his driving test.

His friends congratulated him .... (drive) so well.

f) Sheila makes a lot of money .... (sell) computer software.

She enjoys .... (work) in a big shop.

g) What about .... (have) a drink, Jane?

It's no use .... (wait) any longer.

h) Your answer seems .... (be) wrong, Paul.

You should avoid .... (make) too many mistakes.

JOKE

"Why are you jumping up and down?"
"I've just taken my medicine and I forgot to shake the bottle."

Der to-Infinitiv folgt auf diese Verben:
Es heißt also: *Susan decided **to leave** at ten o'clock.*

to agree	zustimmen	**to manage**	schaffen
to attempt	versuchen	**to offer**	anbieten
to choose	beschließen, wählen	**to plan**	planen
to decide	sich entscheiden	**to promise**	versprechen
to expect	erwarten	**to refuse**	sich weigern
to fail	nicht schaffen	**to seem**	scheinen
to hope	hoffen	**to want**	wollen
I would like	ich möchte		

Die -ing-Form des Verbs folgt auf diese Verben:
Es heißt also: *Susan enjoys play**ing** tennis.*

to avoid	vermeiden	**can't help**	einfach müssen
to carry on	weiterhin tun	**to keep (on)**	weitermachen
to dislike	nicht mögen	**I don't mind**	ich habe nichts dagegen
to enjoy	gern tun	**do you mind ...?**	macht es dir etwas aus ...?
to give up	aufgeben	**to go on**	weitermachen

Nach einigen Verben sind beide Formen möglich:
Es heißt also: *Jason loves watch**ing** TV.* Oder:
*Jason loves **to watch** TV.*

to begin	beginnen	**to like**	gern tun
to continue	weiterhin tun	**to love**	sehr gerne tun
to start	anfangen	**to hate**	nicht mögen, hassen

tipps&tricks

Beachte die unterschiedliche Bedeutung bei *stopp:*
*He stopped **to buy** a newspaper.* (Er hielt an, um eine Zeitung zu kaufen.)
*He stopped **reading** the newspaper.* (Er hörte auf, die Zeitung zu lesen.)

Die -ing-Form folgt nach diesen Verben + Präposition:
Es heißt also: *Paul apologized **for** be**ing** late.*

to apologize for	sich entschuldigen für	**to believe in**	glauben an
to complain about	sich beklagen über	**to decide against**	entscheiden gegen
to dream of/about	träumen von	**to feel like**	Lust haben auf
to look forward to	sich freuen auf	**to object to**	etwas dagegen haben
to rely on	sich verlassen auf	**to succeed in**	Erfolg haben bei/in
to thank for	danken für	**to think of**	denken an

Die -ing-Form nach Adjektivwendungen + Präposition:
Es heißt also: *Susan is fond **of** play**ing** in the school orchestra.*

to be afraid of	Angst haben vor	**to be good at**	gut sein in
to be crazy about	verrückt sein auf/nach	**to be fed up with**	genug haben von
to be famous for	berühmt sein für	**to be interested in**	sich interessieren für
to be keen on	angetan sein von	**to be proud of**	stolz sein auf
to be tired of	es satt haben zu	**to be used to**	gewöhnt sein an

Die -ing-Form nach Substantiven + Präposition:
Es heißt also: *We had no chance **of** winn**ing** the soccer match.*

advantage of	Vorteil des/von	**chance of**	Gelegenheit zu
danger of	Gefahr (zu)	**difficulty (in)**	Schwierigkeit(en) zu/bei
hope of	Hoffnung (auf)	**interest in**	Interesse an
opportunity of	Gelegenheit (zu)	**pleasure of**	Vergnügen (zu)
reason for	Grund für	**time for**	Zeit für
trouble in	Schwierigkeit(en) mit/zu	**way of**	Art und Weise (zu)

Die -ing-Form nach einigen Wendungen:
Es heißt also: *It's no use wait**ing** any longer.*

it's no use	es hat keinen Zweck	**it is worth**	es lohnt sich
How about ...?	wie wär's, wenn ...?	**What about ...?**	wie wär's, wenn ...?

Die -ing-Form nach alleinstehenden Präpositionen:

after leaving	nach dem Weggehen	**before working**	vor dem Arbeiten
by learning	durch Lernen	**instead of eating**	(an)statt zu essen
without speaking	ohne zu sprechen	**on coming**	nach dem Kommen

12 Fill in the correct forms of the words in brackets.

INFO Du übst den etwas schwierigeren Teil einer Aufgabe mit „vermischter Grammatik“: Was tun, wenn mehr als ein Wort in Klammern steht?

a) Jason's parents were angry about their son

They wanted . . . . (Jason, become)

a bank clerk, but he refused.

They also advised . . . . (he, go) to England

to study the language, but he wasn't interested.

b) Jason had different plans.

It was too difficult . . . . (his parents, persuade)

him. It wasn't possible . . . . (they, change)

his mind. Jason said: There is no need . . . . (I, make)

quick decisions.

tipps&tricks Wenn mehr als ein Wort in Klammern steht (Person oder Personalpronomen und ein Verb), bietet sich möglicherweise die Konstruktion *Objekt + to-Infinitiv* bzw. *for + Objekt + to-Infinitiv* an.
Es ist wichtig, dass du die Objektform der Pronomen bildest, z. B.
a) *he → him, they → them.*

13 Some more sentences.

> Du übst Sätze nach dem Muster:
> Verb + Objekt + to-Infinitiv.
>
> INFO

a) The girls wanted to go swimming in the afternoon.

So they persuaded (teacher, give) them no homework.

b) Father didn't allow (Andy, stay out) the whole night.

He wanted (he, be) at home by midnight.

c) Mr Davenport often tells (his pupils, work) harder.

He encourages (they, do) some extra work.

d) Would you like (I, write) the letter for you, Jason?

Oh, yes. But I can't expect (you, do) it on a Sunday.

> Du übst Sätze mit der Konstruktion
> Wort + *for* + Objekt + to-Infinitiv.
>
> INFO

e) There was no need (I, help) my parents.

They had nearly finished their job.

f) Lots of people were waiting (the police, come).

A car had crashed into a shop window.

g) It was too cold (we, swim) in the lake.

So we went to the gymnasium to play volleyball.

h) It was important (Jane, make) that decision.

She couldn't wait much longer.

14 Use the words in brackets in the right form.

INFO Überlege dir, ob du die Adjektive in Klammern übernehmen kannst oder ob du das Adverb davon bilden musst.

a) A woman with a baby in her arms was sitting . . . (sad) in the waiting-room at a railway station, weeping[1] . . . (bitter).

b) Up came a porter[2] and . . . (immediate) asked her what the trouble was.

c) "Oh, dear me," she cried, "some people were in here, and they were so . . . (rude) to me about my son! I'm . . . (total, upset[3]) – they said he looked . . . (ugly).

d) "There, there, my dear," said the porter . . . (kind). "Don't worry about it. I tell you what – how about a . . . (nice) cup of tea?"

e) "You're so . . . (good)," she said, wiping her eyes, "that would be . . . (awful, nice)."
"And while I'm at it," he said, "how about a banana for your monkey?"

1 to weep (weinen) 2 porter (Gepäckträger) 3 upset (betrübt)

tipps&tricks

Du musst überlegen, ob du das Adjektiv (in der richtigen Form) oder das abgeleitete Adverb einsetzt.
Wie **ist** jemand/etwas? → Adjektiv, z. B. c) *they were* ***rude***
Wie **macht** jemand etwas? → Adverb, z. B. *she was sitting* ***sadly***
Wie gut/... ist etwas/jemand? → Adverb, z. B. d) *it is* ***awfully*** *nice*
Wie schlecht/... macht jemand etwas? → Adverb, z. B. *he sings awfully badly.*

She looks ***good*** – Nach bestimmten Verben folgt ein Adjektiv!

15 Adjective or adverb?

a) The new song sounds . . . (real, good).

b) Peter can't pronounce the "th" . . . (correct).

c) The weather is . . . (awful, bad).

d) It is raining . . . (heavy).

e) I tried very . . . (hard) to solve the . . . (difficult) problem.

f) Our soccer team played . . . (extreme, unfair).

tipps&tricks

Entscheide dich zwischen **Adjektiv und Adverb**.

g) The English test looked . . . (easy), but it was . . . (difficult) than we had expected.

h) Sam can play . . . (good) than me. I thought I was the . . . (good) player.

i) Our holiday was . . . (expensive) than last year. It used to be . . . (cheap).

j) The hockey match was . . . (absolutely, boring). It was the . . . (boring) game I've seen this year.

tipps&tricks

Überlege auch die richtige **Form** des Wortes: Grundstufe *(slow/slowly)*, Komparativ *(slower, more slowly)*, Superlativ *(the slowest, the most slowly)*.

JOKE

"Some girls think I'm handsome," said the young Romeo, "and some girls think I'm ugly. What do you think, Ann?" "A bit of both. Pretty ugly."

* pretty = hübsch (adj.), ziemlich (adv.)

Nach diesen Verben, die Zustände oder Eigenschaften beschreiben, folgt ein Adjektiv:

be	sein, werden	**become**	werden
feel	sich fühlen	**get**	werden
grow	werden	**look**	aussehen
seem	scheinen	**smell**	riechen
sound	klingen	**taste**	schmecken

16 Put into reported speech.

JOKE

Teacher: "Geoff, why were you absent from school yesterday?"
Geoff: "I wasn't well, Miss. I had a bit of a temperature."
Teacher: "I see. And do you have a note from your mother or your father?"
Geoff: "No, Miss."
Teacher: "I shall expect to see one tomorrow."
Geoff: "Yes, Miss."
Next day Geoff handed in the following note: "Dear Miss, Geoff was absent from school on Toosday because of a coald*."*
Yours faithfully,
My Father

**(Geoff unterliefen einige Rechtschreibfehler: Tuesday, cold)*

a) The teacher asked Geoff . . .;
b) Geoff answered that . . .
c) The teacher wanted to know . . .
d) Geoff replied . . .
e) The teacher went on . . .
f) Geoff promised . . .
g) In the note you could read that Geoff . . .

tipps&tricks

Da die einleitenden Verben *(reporting verbs)* im **past tense** stehen (z. B. *asked, answered, said*), musst du die **Zeitenverschiebung** berücksichtigen, z. B. *present* → *past*: *will* → *would*. Denke auch an die normale **Wortstellung** in indirekten Fragesätzen und Besonderheiten bei der Bildung von indirekten **Bitten und Befehlen** (z. B. He told me *to go*, he asked her *not to leave*).

Reported speech (Indirekte Rede)

Wandelst du die direkte Rede in indirekte Rede um, musst du folgende Veränderungen beachten:

Wenn das ***reporting verb*** (= einleitendes Verb) im ***present*** (z. B. *says*) oder ***present perfect*** (z. B. *has said*) steht, bleiben die Zeiten gleich. Die **Pronomen** werden sinngemäß verändert.

Bei der **indirekten Frage** übernimmst du das Fragewort der direkten Rede (z. B. *where*).

Indirekte Yes/No-Fragen werden mit ***if*** oder ***whether*** (– ob) gebildet. Normale Wortstellung (S-P-O) bei der indirekten Frage!

Steht das ***reporting verb*** (= einleitende Verb) im ***past*** (z. B. *asked*) oder ***past perfect*** (z. B. *had asked*), **verändern sich**, zusätzlich zu den Pronomen, **auch die Zeiten:** *present → past; past → past/past perfect; present perfect → past perfect; future → conditional; future perfect → conditional perfect*

Die **Modalverben** verändern sich wie folgt: *will → would, may → might; must → had to; needn't → didn't have to; can → could*

Could, should, would, might werden nicht verändert.

Ein **Befehl** wird mit **tell + Objekt + to-Infinitiv** ausgedrückt (z. B. *told Sam to ...*).

Über eine **Bitte** wird mit **ask + Objekt + to-Infinitiv** berichtet (z. B. *asked her to ...*).

Weitere Veränderungen bei der Umwandlung von **direkter** in **indirekte** Rede: *this → that; these → those; here → there; today → that day; yesterday → the day before; tomorrow → the next/following day; last month → the previous month; a year ago → a year before*

17 Rewrite the sentences replacing the participles with different kinds of clauses.

INFO: Du formst die Partizipien *(participles)* in Relativsätze bzw. Nebensätze um.

a) Some youngsters frightened the travellers waiting for their train.

....

b) There was a complete silence broken only by the train.

....

c) After doing his homework, Tom went to bed.

....

d) Feeling it would be very cold outside, Jane put on her coat.

....

e) John went to the doctor hoping to get help.

....

f) There was a little girl sitting opposite us.

....

g) Andrew wrote to his brother wanting to give him his new address.

....

h) Cricket is a game played in England and Australia.

....

tipps&tricks: Überlege, welcher Relativsatz bzw. Nebensatz vom Sinn her passt, z. B. a) travellers *who* were waiting = Relativsatz mit aktiver Form), b) silence *which/that* was broken = Relativsatz mit passiver Form, c) *After* he had done = Nebensatz der Zeit, d) *As* she felt = Nebensatz des Grundes, e) *and* hoped = zweiter Satz.

Participial constructions (Partizipsätze)

Verschiedene Satzkonstruktionen können durch ein **Partizip** verkürzt werden:

1. **Relativsätze** (relative clauses)

*The boy **who lives** next to John is my friend.*
→ *The boy **living** next to John is my friend.*

*I bought a book **which was written** by Agatha Christie.*
→ *I bought a book **written** by Agatha Christie.*

-ing-Form (z. B. *living*): aktiver Sinn
Partizip Perfekt (z. B. *written*): passiver Sinn

2. **Nebensätze der Zeit** (clauses of time)

***When** John **saw** the taxi he stopped it at once.*
→ ***When seeing** the taxi, John stopped it at once.*

***After he had arrived** home, he paid the driver.*
→ ***Having arrived** (Arriving) home, he paid the driver.*

Die Konjunktionen *when*, *while*, *before* bleiben erhalten, *after* kann wegfallen.

3. **Nebensätze des Grundes** (clauses of reason)

***As he was** tired John went to bed.*
→ ***Being** tired John went to bed.*

*John could not sleep **because there was** a loud noise.*
→ *John could not sleep **being** a loud noise there.*

Die Konjunktionen *as*, *because*, *since* fallen weg.

4. **Hauptsätze**, die mit *and* verbunden sind:

*John went to bed **and hoped** to sleep immediately.*
→ *John went to bed **hoping** to sleep immediately.*

Die Konjunktion *and* fällt weg.

4. Guided writing

INFO

Du sollst mithilfe der englischen Informationen und der Piktogramme (Bildzeichen) einen kleinen Text verfassen *(guided writing)*.

Your family probably cannot afford a holiday at a Hilton hotel, but your parents have seen an interesting little advertisement in an English Tourist Board brochure:

SEAVIEW HOTEL
Owners: Mr and Mrs D. Murray
19-21 Albany Street
Eastbourne
comfortable family-run hotel, 11 rooms,

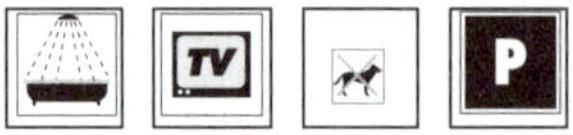

1 What do the signs mean? Write complete sentences.

a) This means . . . .

. . . .

b) You . . . .

. . . .

c) The hotel . . . .

. . . .

d) You are not . . . .

. . . .

tipps&tricks

Schreibe vollständige Sätze *(Write complete sentences)* und achte vor allem auf den grammatikalisch richtigen Satzanschluss an die vorgegebenen Teile und die richtige Wortstellung.

INFO

Du sollst mithilfe der englischen Stichwörter eine Situation schildern.

2 **How to help an old lady.**

Use these items: *yesterday – walk – Park Lane – see – old lady – carry – big bag – ask – help – polite young man – carry – bag – house – thank.*

. . . .

. . . .

. . . .

. . . .

. . . .

. . . .

. . . .

. . . .

tipps&tricks

Die Geschichte passierte gestern, d. h., du verwendest *past tense*, wobei du überlegst, ob *simple past* oder *past progressive* notwendig sind.
Beachte höfliche Umgangsformen *(a polite young man),* wenn du die Fragen bildest bzw. Reaktionen wiedergibst.

INFO

Du sollst die Situation im *cartoon* beschreiben und deine Schlüsse daraus ziehen.

3 **Describe the situation in the cartoon and say what its message is. Write at least 50 words.**

tipps&tricks

Schreibe mindestens 50 Wörter *(write at least 50 words)* und vergiss nicht, außer der Situation auch die Folgerung sprachlich wiederzugeben. Warum ist die Lage so dramatisch? Wen ruft der Mann wohl an?

Du sollst einen Lückendialog *(defective dialogue)* vervollständigen. Du verwendest die vorgegebenen Teile (Aussagen, Fragen) und die Informationen aus dem Bild.

iNFO

Paul and Linda are in front of a cinema:

4. Complete their conversation.

a) P: "Look – there's an Elvis film on: 'King Creole!'

. . . . ?"

b) L: "No, I haven't. . . . . ?"

P: "It's got plenty of music and a lot of action."

c) L: "It sounds good.. . . . . ?"

. . . .

P: "A singer in New Orleans who makes his living as a cleaner in a night club. It's supposed to be Elvis' best film."

d) L: "It certainly sounds interesting. . . . ."

. . . .

e) P: "You mean right now? Well, I'm afraid I can't, because . . . ."

. . . .

f) L: "What a pity.. . . . . ?"

g) P: "Tomorrow evening? Sorry, but . . . .

either, because. . . . ."

tipps&tricks

Lies den vorliegenden Teil des Dialogs im Ganzen mehrmals durch. Dort findest du Hinweise für deine Lösung, z. B. a) Die Zeit deiner Frage muss der Antwort von b) *I haven't* entsprechen; bei d) lässt die Antwort von e) *You mean right now? Well, I'm afraid I can't...* auf eine nette Einladung schließen; bei e) und g) sollte dir ein Grund einfallen, warum Paul leider (*I'm afraid, sorry*) keine Zeit hat.

INFO

Du sollst ein Telefongespräch vollständig wiedergeben.

5 Complete the telephone call between Paul and Jane.

a) J: . . . .
P: Paul. Hello, Jane.

b) J: . . . .
P: I'm very well, thanks.

c) J: . . . .
P: I'm just doing my maths homework.

d) J:. . . . . ?
P: No, it's quite difficult.

e) J:. . . . . ?
P: I don't think, I'll finish it until five o'clock.

f) J:. . . . . ?
P: No, I'm afraid we can't meet at the café this afternoon.

g) J:. . . . . ?
P: Yes, on Sunday it would be nice.

h) J:. . . . . ?
P: I'd say three o'clock would be all right.

i) J:. . . . . ?
P: No, you needn't. I'll come by bike.

j) J:. . . . . ?
P: I must be home by nine.

k) J: . . . .
P: Cheerio.

tipps&tricks

Auch bei dieser Aufgabe liest du zunächst den ganzen Dialog in Ruhe durch. Dann überlegst du dir, welche Redemittel für ein Telefongespräch notwendig sind, z. B. a) Wie beginnst du einen Anruf (Gruß? Name?), b) Wie fragst du nach dem Wohlbefinden, c) Du stellst deine Frage entsprechend der Antwort *I'm just doing*, d) Du erkennst aus der Antwort *No*, dass du eine Entscheidungsfrage (ohne Fragewort) stellen musst, k) Du überlegst dir ein freundliches Abschiedswort.

6 Complete the interview.

Here are the answers given by Mrs McGregor (M).
You are the interviewer (I).

a) I: " . . . . "?
M: "I'm a secretary."

b) I: " . . . . "?
M: "I live near Manchester, in a small village."

c) I: " . . . . "?
M: "No, it isn't very far from the centre. About eight miles."

d) I: " . . . . "?
M: "By train. It only takes me half an hour to reach the office."

e) I: " . . . . "?
M: "Yes, I like my job very much. It's interesting."

f) I: " . . . . "?
M: "Well, I usually start work at quarter past nine."

g) I: " . . . . "?
M: "My husband? He's a policeman."

h) I: " . . . . "?
M: "Oh, yes. We've two daughters and a son."

i) I: " . . . . "?
M: "The girls are sixteen and fourteen, and the boy is twenty-one."

j) I: "Thank you very much, Mrs McGregor."

M: ". . . . ."

tipps&tricks

Bilde die Frage aus der *gesamten* Antwort, z. B. b) *Where do you live?* – frage also nicht nach den einzelnen Angaben, wie *Do you live near Manchester and is it a small village?* Antworten mit *Yes* oder *No* verlangen eine Entscheidungsfrage (ohne Fragewort!), z. B. c) Wie reagierst du auf einen *Dank*, z. B. j)?

How to ask questions:	How to give answers:
a) personal questions	
What's your name?	I'm Adam./My name is Susan White.
Where do you live?	I live in Macclesfield.
What's your job?	I work at a bank./I'm a shop assistant.
b) age	
How old are you?	I'm sixteen./I'll be seventeen next month.
What's your age?	
c) price	
How much is this?	It's £ 2.50.
How much are these shoes?	They're £ 45.
How much does it cost?	It costs two hundred pounds.
d) size	
What size is this dress?	It's size 8.
What size are these shoes?	They're size ... .
e) appearance	
What is he/she like?	He/She's friendly and funny.
What does he/she look like?	He/she's slim and tall.
What does she wear?	She wears a blue T-shirt and green jeans.
What is she wearing?	She's wearing a black skirt.
f) colour	
What colour is the dress?	It's red.
What colour are the curtains?	They're blue with red stripes.
g) shape	
What shape is the van?	It's square.
How long is the bridge?	It's two hundred metres long.
How wide is the river?	It's a hundred metres wide.
h) opening and closing hours	
When does the café open?	It opens at nine a.m.
When do the pubs close?	They close at eleven p.m.

INFO

Du sollst ein Gespräch in direkter Rede *(in direct speech)* wiedergeben. Deutsche Informationen leiten deinen Dialog *(guided dialogue)*.

You have had a bad cough for several months now, so you decide to see a doctor.

7 Write down the dialogue in direct speech.

Der Arzt fragt, was dir fehlt.

a) Doc.: " . . . . ?"
Du erzählst ihm, dass du seit Monaten Husten hast und ihn nicht loswirst.

b) You: ". . . . . "
Er will wissen, ob du starker Raucher bist.

c) Doc.: " . . . . ?"
Du bejahst dies und sagst dann, dass du gewöhnlich fünf bis zehn Zigaretten am Tag rauchst, gelegentlich aber auch fünfzehn.

d) You: ". . . . . "
Er fragt, ob dir klar ist, dass Rauchen äußerst ungesund ist.

e) Doc.: " . . . . ?"
Du erwiderst, dass dir das egal ist, weil du ja noch jung bist.

f) You: ". . . . . "
Er will wissen, ob du jemals versucht hast, das Rauchen aufzugeben.

g) Doc.: " . . . . ?"
Du erzählst ihm, dass du es schon zweimal versucht hast, dass du es aber nicht geschafft hast.

h) You: "Well, ... "
Doc.: "I can help you there."

tipps&tricks

Natürlich kannst du nicht wörtlich übersetzen. Du musst dich vielmehr in die Rolle der Sprecher (Arzt, du als Patient/in) versetzen und die Reaktionen, Empfindungen, Zweifel in Worte fassen, z. B. c) Du *bejahst* dies, Kurzantwort auf die Frage *Are you a strong smoker?*, f) *Er will wissen, ob* ... Du stellst eine direkte Frage *Hast du jemals versucht ... ?*

8 Write down the conversation in direct speech.

Ian trifft seinen Freund Geoff und sie unterhalten sich über ihre Ferien.

INFO Du sollst ihre Unterhaltung in direkter Rede wiedergeben.

a) Ian begrüßt Jeff.

b) Jeff erwidert den Gruß und fügt hinzu, dass er Ian schon lange nicht gesehen hat.

c) Ian will von Jeff wissen, wo er seine letzten Ferien verbracht hat.

d) Jeff antwortet, dass er zuerst in Wales war und dann nach Kanada geflogen ist. Er fragt Ian, ob er ihm Fotos zeigen soll.

e) Ian bejaht dies und meint, dass er sie sehr gern sehen würde. Er fragt, wann sie sich denn treffen könnten.

f) Jeff zögert kurz und antwortet, der beste Tag wäre der nächste Samstag um 18 Uhr bei sich zu Hause.

g) Ian möchte wissen, ob er seine Schwester mitbringen kann. Sie interessiere sich sehr für Kanada.

h) Jeff stimmt selbstverständlich zu und fügt hinzu, dass er sich auf das Treffen freut.

tipps&tricks Lies den Bericht sorgfältig durch. Versetze dich dann in die Rolle von Ian und Jeff und denke daran, dass du nicht wörtlich übersetzen kannst, z. B. *Ian begrüßt Jeff, Ian fragt Jeff, Ian bejaht dies, Ian zögert kurz.*
Du wendest vielmehr deine Sprachmuster an: a) und b) Wie begrüßen sich Freunde? e) Kurzantwort mit *Yes* auf eine Frage. f) Zögern kannst du mit *Well* oder *Let me see* ausdrücken. Denke an Signalwörter für die Zeiten, z. B. b) *lange (Zeit)* nicht → present perfect, c) letzte Ferien → simple past.

9 **Give the conversation.**

Gib die Unterhaltung zwischen Mr Ward und dem Angestellten in einem Reisebüro wieder. Verwende auch die Informationen aus dem englischen Text. INFO

Mr Ward and his wife are planning a trip to the Continent in August. They want to take their car with them. They'd prefer to take a ferry overnight. They'd arrive on the Continent in the morning. They know that if they travel in August, they must book in advance.
Mr Ward goes to a travel office in Manchester, where he lives. The travel agent (T.A.) suggests the shortest way.

a)	T.A. fragt, was er für ihn tun kann.	Mr W. sagt, dass er eine Reise zum Kontinent plant.
b)	T.A. sagt, der kürzeste Weg sei von Manchester nach Hull.	Mr W. fragt, ob von Hull eine Fähre zum Kontinent geht.
c)	T.A. antwortet, dass die Fähre um 18.00 Uhr abfährt und direkt nach Ostende oder Rotterdam fährt.	Mr W. sagt, dass er Ostende vorzieht, weil sie noch Brüssel besuchen könnten. Er fragt, wie teuer die Fähre für zwei Personen und ein Auto sei.
d)	T.A. antwortet, dass die einfache Fahrt mit einer Kabine ungefähr £ 180,– kostet.	Mr W. sagt, dass diese Strecke die beste für sie sei, weil sie nicht durch ganz England mit dem Auto fahren müssten. Er fragt, ob sie die Fähre im August im Voraus buchen müssten.
e)	T.A. antwortet, dass es notwendig sei, weil viele Leute in diesem Monat reisen.	Mr W. sagt, dass er die Hin- und Rückfahrt buchen wird und dass er die Fahrkarten gleich bezahlen möchte.
f)	T.A. bedankt sich und wünscht ihnen einen schönen Urlaub.	

Begrüßung – Persönliche Fragen – Vorschläge machen

Du begrüßt jemanden:	Hallo/Servus Guten Morgen, Herr Brown. Guten Abend, Paul. (Gruß am Nachmittag) Guten Tag. Wie geht's? Danke, sehr gut. Ganz gut. Servus/Tschüs Auf Wiedersehen, Mrs White. Auf bald.	Hello/Hi Good morning, Mr Brown. Good evening, Paul. Good afternoon. How do you do? How are you? Very well, thank you. Not too bad. Bye/Cheerio Good-bye, Mrs White. See you later.
Du stellst persönliche Fragen:	Du fragst nach dem Namen, dem Alter, der Wohnung, ob er/sie Geschwister hat, an welche Schule er/sie geht, ob er/sie diese mag, welches die Lieblingsfächer sind, was er/sie am Wochenende macht.	What's your name? How old are you? Where do you live? Have you any brothers and sisters? Which school do you go to? Do you like school? Which are your favourite subjects? What do you do at weekends?
Du schlägst etwas vor:	Du schlägst vor, dass ihr ins Kino geht, etwas trinkt, sofort mit etwas anfangt, viel Spaß miteinander habt.	Shall we go to the cinema? What about having a drink? I'd suggest starting at once. Let's have a good time.

Nach dem Weg fragen und Auskunft erteilen – Etwas (gern) haben

Du fragst nach dem Weg oder gibst Auskunft:	Du fragst jemanden ...	
	ob er dir den Weg nach ... sagen kann,	Can you tell me the way to ... please?
	(du entschuldigst dich dabei für die Störung!)	Excuse me, can you tell me the way to ...?
	Du antwortest, ...	
	dass er/sie geradeaus gehen soll,	Yes, go straight on here.
	dass er/sie am Kino vorbeigehen soll,	Go past the cinema.
	dass er/sie an der Ampel nach links abbiegen soll,	Turn left at the traffic lights.
	dass er/sie an der nächsten Kreuzung links/rechts abbiegen soll,	Take the next turning on the left/right.
	dass er/sie die zweite Querstraße nach links einbiegen soll.	Take the second turning on the left.
	Du bedankst dich ...	Thank you/Thank you very much.
	(sehr) und drückst deine Freude aus.	Thanks awfully. You're so kind.
	Der andere sagt darauf, ... Gern geschehen.	You're welcome/Don't mention it/Not at all.
Du magst etwas (nicht):	Du sagst, dass du Rock (sehr) magst,	I love Rock/I like it very much.
	Tennis toll findest,	Tennis is great.
	Cricket sei in Ordnung,	Cricket is all right/okay.
	aus Hockey machst du dir wenig,	I don't really mind hockey.
	Partys sind langweilig,	Parties are boring.
	Schule ist nicht interessant,	Lessons aren't interesting.
	Tests verabscheust du, und	I hate tests./I don't like them at all.
	Wörter lernen ist furchtbar.	Learning vocabulary is awful.

10 Write a letter to an English boy or girl.
Use the information given in the exercise.

INFO
Du sollst einen Brief an einen Jugendlichen in England schreiben, der vielleicht dein zukünftiger Brieffreund wird. Achte auf die besondere Form eines Briefes: Anschrift, Anrede, Schluss.

(your address)
. . . .
. . . .
. . . .
. . . .

. . . .

My name is . . . .

I live in . . . . I would like . . . .

. . . . My hobbies are . . . .

. . . . I don't like . . . .

My father is. . . . . and my mother . . . .

. . . .

My school is in . . . .

In our class there are . . . .

I go to school from . . . . to . . . .

On . . . . we have no school.

I hope to . . . .

With . . . .

. . . .

tipps&tricks
Beachte die Form eines Briefes: Anschrift, passende Anrede (bei Freunden: *Dear ...*), ein kurzer Einleitungsgedanke (wie du heißt), der Hauptteil (Du erzählst ein wenig über dich, deine Interessen, Familie und Schulklasse), ein abschließender Gedanke (Hoffen auf baldige Antwort) und ein Schlusswort.

11 **Write a postcard using the following information.**

Gabi's boy-friend Peter is in London. He is writing a postcard from there. Use the following information to write this postcard.

Address: Gabi Hollbeck, Neckarweg 17, 70376 Stuttgart

here in London/three days now – weather beautiful
visit/Tower, Hyde Park, Big Ben – ferry/Ostend/Saturday
look forward/see you

tipps&tricks

Achte auf die richtigen Zeiten, z. B. a) *here + 3 days now* → present perfect, d) *(next) Saturday* → future, e) Was folgt nach *look forward?*

INFO Du verfasst ein Bewerbungsschreiben für eine Au-pair-Stelle in England. Die Adresse stammt aus einer Tageszeitung.

12 Use the following information to write Susanne's letter of application.

Susanne Meister (18) wants to be an au-pair girl in England.
She lives in 70489 Stuttgart, Zaungasse 3.
She is writing to Mrs Ashton whose address she got from an advertisement in the "Stuttgarter Zeitung" last Saturday.
Susanne left secondary school at sixteen. She was employed at a kindergarten for one year.
Then she studied another year at a technical high school.
She visited England last year and wants to spend there more time to improve her English. She intends to study social science after the year in England.
She hopes to receive a reply quite soon.

. . . .

. . . .

. . . .

. . . .

. . . .

. . . .

. . . .

. . . .

. . . .

. . . .

. . . .

. . . .

tipps&tricks

Versetze dich in Susannes Lage und bewerbe dich um die Stelle. Bedenke, dies ist ein etwas offizielleres Schreiben an eine unbekannte erwachsene Person und berücksichtige dies: Anrede, Schluss, Gruß.

Absender	14, Brynton Road Macclesfield England, SK 10 3 AF	!!! zuerst die Hausnummer !!! Postleitzahl
Datum	April 1st May 2nd June 25th	1. April 2. Mai 25. Juni
Anrede	Dear Tom Dear Uncle Geoff Dear Mrs Appleby Dear Mr Orwell Dear Sir/Dear Sirs	Lieber Tom Lieber Onkel Geoff Liebe Frau Appleby (bei Bekannten) Sehr geehrter Herr Orwell (Geschäftsbrief) Sehr geehrte/r Herr(en) (Geschäftsbrief)
Einleitung	Many thanks for your letter I'm sorry I haven't written earlier. I want to apologize for ...	Vielen Dank für deinen Brief Leider habe ich nicht früher schreiben können. Ich möchte mich entschuldigen, dass...
Grund	I'd like to invite you We'd like to spend I want to apply for	Ich möchte dich einladen Wir möchten ... verbringen Ich möchte mich um ... bewerben
Schluss	I'm looking forward to I hope to hear from you I hope you will answer Please remember me to Best wishes to you and	Ich freue mich darauf, ... Hoffentlich höre ich von dir Ich hoffe, Sie werden ... antworten Empfehlen Sie mich bitte Die besten Grüße an dich und
Unterschrift	Lots of love Love, Tina Yours, Tom Yours sincerely, Clara Yours faithfully, John F. Myer	Liebe Grüße in Liebe, Tina Dein Tom Mit freundlichen Grüßen, Clara (Bekannte) Mit vorzüglicher Hochachtung, John F. Myer (bei Geschäftsbriefen)

5. Translation

INFO

Du übersetzt einen längeren Text, der sich inhaltlich an den Comprehension Test anlehnt.

1 Translate into German.

Now you are the proud owner of a pair of quality shoes.
By buying Dr Martens you have made the right choice.

They are worn by young and old, by bankers as much as by policemen, by rock stars and nurses. They last a long time and are fashionable all year round.

Of course, our shoes and boots have been copied again and again. These *imitations*[1] look similar; only when you wear them you realise that they are not the same. You will soon find out how well the real "DMs" protect your feet from the cold, mud and snow. Their soft leather and thick rubber soles are unbeatable.

Although it is easy to take care of your "DMs", you should follow the *instructions*[1] below:
- Remove dirt with a damp cloth.
- Apply shoe polish or wax occasionally, and your shoes will look as good as the day you first saw them.

1 *Die schräg gedruckten Wörter sollen nicht mit einem Fremdwort übersetzt werden.*

tipps&tricks

Lies den Text mehrmals durch und kennzeichne schwierige Wörter und Konstruktionen. Besonders problematische Stellen solltest du in einer *Rohübersetzung* auf einem Konzeptblatt vorbereiten. Bemühe dich um gute Formulierungen und versuche, unbekannte Wörter aus dem Sinnzusammenhang heraus zu erschließen. Es ist wichtig, dass du kein Wort und schon gar keinen Satz auslässt: Für jeden Satz ist eine gewisse Punktzahl vorgesehen, von der pro Fehler je 1 Punkt abgezogen wird.

Da du mit der Übersetzung eine Menge Punkte erreichen kannst*, lohnt es sich bestimmt, dieses Kapitel genau durchzuarbeiten. Bearbeite die folgenden Übersetzungen, die jeweils einzelne Schwierigkeiten enthalten. Auch hier kannst du natürlich persönliche Schwerpunkte setzen.

* nach Prüfung und Bundesland verschieden.

INFO

5.1 Erschließe einzelne unbekannte („vergessene" oder wirklich fremde) **Wörter.**
Du kennst das Grundwort, z. B. *to beat* (schlagen) und folgerst *unbeatable (unschlagbar);* du kennst *to choose* (wählen) und übersetzt *choice* (Wahl); du kennst die Vorsilbe *ex-* (aus-) und erschließt *exit* (Ausgang).

5.2 Halte problematische Wörter auseinander.
sog. *falsche Freunde*, wie etwa to *become* (werden/nicht: bekommen!), *boot* (Stiefel/nicht: Boot!).
- *kleine Wörter*, wie z. B. *of course* (natürlich), *although* (obwohl), *also* (auch), *always* (immer), *already* (schon), *almost* (fast).
- *Wörter mit Mehrfachbedeutungen*, z. B. *last* (hier: halten/oft: letzter), *apply* (hier: auftragen/auch: sich bewerben).
- Traue dich, *frei* zu *übersetzen*, z. B. She *likes* wearing boots (Sie trägt *gerne* Stiefel).

5.3 Übersetze Zeiten angemessen.
- I *have had* these boots for two months
  (Ich *habe* diese Stiefel *schon* seit zwei Monaten).

5.4 Achte auf Modalverben.
- you *should* follow (du *solltest* befolgen/nicht: du sollst)
  you *mustn't* forget to remove dirt (du *darfst nicht* vergessen, ...)

5.5 Überlege dir schwierige Konstruktionen:
-ing-Formen (Gerund)
- by *buying* ... *(Durch den Kauf .../Wenn du kaufst, ...)*

Partizipien
- *When following* the instructions *(Wenn du* die Gebrauchsanleitung *befolgst)*

Infinitivsätze
- I want *you to buy these shoes* (Ich will, *dass du ... kaufst*).

2 **Translate the words in bold print.**

JOKE

At the scene of a bank raid the police sergeant came running up to his inspector and ***exclaimed****, "He got away, sir!"*
The inspector was furious.
"But I told you to put a man on all ***exits****!" he roared.*
"How could he have got away?"
"He left by one of the entrances, sir!"

tipps&tricks

Die Vorsilbe ex- bedeutet oft aus- („Ex" heißt, z. B. austrinken!): *exclaim* – ausrufen und *exit* – Ausgang werden für dich zum Heimspiel!

3 **Words with the prefixes ex- and im-/in-/irr-**

tipps&tricks

***ex**pression*	***im**pression*
Ausdruck	**Ein**druck

Du kannst auf diese Weise zahlreiche, auch unbekannte Vokabeln selbstständig übersetzen.

a) to express
b) to export
c) extreme
d) extraordinary
e) expense
f) exhibition
g) exchange visit
h) excellent
i) to impress
j) to import
k) inhabitant
l) to immigrate
m) immigration
n) immigrant

!

ex-wife (ehemalige Ehefrau)
ex-president (ehemaliger Präsident)

impolite (unhöflich): Beachte, dass **im-** auch das Gegenteil des Grundwortes (polite) bedeuten kann.

4 **Translate.**

tipps&tricks

happy (glücklich)	**un**happy (unglücklich)
patient (geduldig)	**im**patient (ungeduldig)
to like (mögen)	to **dis**like (nicht mögen)

Wörter mit den Vorsilben **un-, im-/in-/irr-** bzw. **dis-** bedeuten häufig *das Gegenteil* des Grundwortes.

a) insecure
b) impolite
c) independent
d) rregular
e) invisible
f) impossible
g) incorrect
h) inefficient
i) inexpensive
j) informal

k) unusual
l) unbeatable
m) unbelievable
n) uncertain
o) unconscious
p) uncountable
q) to undress
r) unemployment

s) to disagree
t) disagreement
u) disadvantage
v) dishonest
w) to disobey
x) dissatisfied

tipps&tricks

to build (bauen)	to **re**build (wiederaufbauen)
to write (schreiben)	to **re**write (neu schreiben)

Die Vorsilbe **re-** bedeutet oft wieder/neu.

a) to recycle
b) to reconsider
c) to reconstruct
d) to replay
e) to rewind
f) to reorganize

Leider gibt es halt immer Ausnahmen,
z. B. bei: to *re*ceive (bekommen)
to *re*port (berichten)
to *dis*cuss (erörtern)

!

5 **Translate.**

a) Jason wants to *become* a teacher for primary school.

. . . .

b) Sarah worked so hard that she *eventually* was ill.

. . . .

c) Andrew saw a *snake* by the door.

. . . .

d) Before Billy went to the *gymnasium*, he had bought a *map*.

. . . .

tipps&tricks

Du darfst hier nicht so ohne weiteres drauflosübersetzen! Natürlich heißt es nicht: Jason will einen Lehrer für die Grundschule *bekommen*, sondern er will Lehrer **werden**.
Sarah arbeitete nicht so schwer, dass sie *eventuell* krank wurde, sondern sie wurde **schließlich** krank.
Andrew sah keine *Schnecke* an der Tür, sondern eine **Schlange**.
Billy ging nicht ins *Gymnasium*, sondern in die Turnhalle und er kaufte keine *Mappe*, sondern eine Landkarte.

Präge dir die wichtigsten dieser „falschen Freunde“ (false friends) auf der nächsten Seite ein.

	richtig übersetzt	Dies sind die „falschen Freunde“!	
actual	wirklich, tatsächlich	aktuell	topical, current
also	auch	also	so, therefore
art	Kunst	Art	way, kind, sort
bank	Bank/Ufer	(Sitz-)Bank	bench
to become	werden	bekommen	get, receive
biscuit	Keks, Plätzchen	Biskuit	sponge biscuit
blame	tadeln	blamieren jd.	show sb. up
boot	Stiefel	Boot	boat
brave	tapfer	brav	good (a ~ boy)
briefcase	Aktentasche	Brieftasche	wallet
circle	Kreis	Zirkel	compasses
college	Hochschule	Kollege	colleague
costly	teuer, kostspielig	köstlich	delicious
critic	Kritiker	Kritik	criticism
crowd	(Menschen-)Menge	Kraut	cabbage
eventually	schließlich	eventuell	perhaps, possibly
fast	schnell	fast	almost, nearly
floor	Fußboden, Stockwerk	Flur	corridor, hall
gift	Geschenk	Gift	poison
go on	weitermachen, weiter-	hinaufgehen	go up
gymnasium	Turnhalle	Gymnasium	grammar school
hose	Schlauch	Hose	trousers

	richtig übersetzt	Dies sind die „falschen Freunde“!	
kind	Art und Weise	Kind	child
lecture	Vortrag	Lektüre	reading matter
local	örtlich	Lokal	pub
look forward to	sich freuen auf	nach vorn schauen	look forward
map	Landkarte	Mappe	satchel
marmalade	Orangenmarmelade	Marmelade	jam
meaning	Bedeutung	Meinung	opinion
mist	Nebel	Mist	manure
murder	Mord	Mörder	murderer
note	Notiz, Banknote	Note, Zensur	mark
novel	Roman	Novelle	novella
physician	Arzt	Physiker	physicist
prospect	Aussicht	Prospekt	leaflet
receipt	Quittung	Rezept	recipe
rent	Miete	Rente	pension
salad	Salat (Gericht)	Salat (Kopf-)	lettuce
sensible	vernünftig	sensibel	sensitive
snake	Schlange	Schnecke	snail
spend	ausgeben, verbringen	spenden	give, donate
stadium	Stadion	Stadium	stage
starve	verhungern	sterben	die
stay	bleiben	stehen	stand
stream	Bach	Strom, Fluss	river
strong	stark	streng	strict
the other day	neulich	am anderen Tag	on the other day

6 **Translate the words in bold print.**

JOKE

A lodger was complaining about the food to his landlady.
*"I did***n't** *like that pie* **at all***, Mrs Pierce."*
Mrs Pierce was furious. "I've been making pies since before you were born," she said angrily.
*"***Perhaps** *that was one of them," said the lodger feelingly.*

tipps&tricks

Diese „kleinen Wörter" können dich – gerade beim Prüfungsstress – oft ganz schön nerven.

Some more words.

a) above b) ago
c) almost d) already
e) always f) although
g) at last h) at least
i) ever j) however
k) not ... either l) not ... yet

immer
schon einmal

auch nicht
noch nicht

schließlich
mindestens

vor
über

fast
schon

jedoch
obwohl

7 **Translate the words in bold print.**

JOKE

"Do you notice any change in me?"
"No, why?"
"I've just swallowed a penny."

tipps&tricks

Hast du gezögert, wie du *change* übersetzen sollst? Es hat ja viele unterschiedliche Bedeutungen: *Veränderung – Wechselgeld – sich umziehen – verändern – umsteigen*. Sicher hast du *Veränderung* geschrieben und dich nicht durch "penny" verwirren lassen.

Some more words with more than one meaning.

a) This record is **for** Susan.
I've been learning English **for** six years now.
We use a dictionary **for** looking up words.
Is this the train **for** Glasgow?
You should take something **for** your cold.
The man was arrested **for** theft.

b) The time went **by** slowly.
I'll be home **by** eleven o'clock.
The thief was caught **by** the police.
Susan won the prize **by** writing an essay.
I usually go to school **by** bus.
Grandpa is sitting **by** the window.

c) The book is **on** the table.
There is a picture **on** the wall.
We came here **on** the train.
I go to school **on** foot.
I was glad **on** getting your letter.
I saw a show **on** TV.
I've got no money **on** me.
What's **on** at the cinema?
The girl shouted at Jack, but he walked **on**.

d) Can you show me the **way** to the cinema?
Look this **way**.
Peter always does things his **way**.
The best **way** to learn English is to go to England for some time.
It's a long **way** to Tipperary.
Which **way** is the church from here? – To the north.
Give **way** to traffic coming from the left.
Let's do it the other **way** round.
I like his **way** of life.

e) I don't understand what you **mean**.
What does this sign **mean**?
One word may have several different **meanings**.
It was only **meant** as a joke.
He is so **mean** to his brother.
Which **means of transport** do you like best?

f) **Use** the words in brackets.
Grandfather **used to** live in that house.
I'm not **used to** getting up early.
The **use** of a calculator is not allowed.
What's the **use** of this machine?
It's no use waiting any longer.

Halte auseinander:
to use
I'm used to + -ing-Form
he **used to** + Infinitiv

g) **spare** time. . . . .

spare wheel . . . .

Can you **spare** me a moment? . . . .

spare: ~ '**part** *n.* Ersatzteil, *das;* ~ '**tyre** *n.* **a)** Reserve-, Ersatzreifen, *der;* **b)** *(Brit. fig. coll.)* Rettungsring, *der (ugs.);* ~ '**wheel** *n.* Ersatzrad, *das*
sparing ['speərɪŋ] *adj.* sparsam; **be ~ of sth./in the use of sth.** mit etw. sparsam umgehen
spark [spɑ:k] **1.** *n.* **a)** Funke, *der;* **the ~s [begin to] fly** *(fig.)* es funkt *(ugs.);* **a ~ of generosity/decency** *(fig.)* ein Funke[n] Großzügigkeit/Anstand; **b)** *(in sparking-plug)* Zündfunke[n], *der (Kfz-W.);* **c) a bright ~** *(clever person; also iron.)* ein schlauer Kopf. **2.** *v.t. see* **~ off**
~ **'off** *v.t.* **a)** *(cause to explode)* zünden; **b)** *(fig.: start)* auslösen
'**sparking-plug** *n.* *(Brit. Motor Veh.)* Zündkerze, *die*
sparkle ['spɑ:kl] **1.** *v.i.* **a)** *(flash)* ‹*Tautropfen:*› glitzern; ‹*Augen:*› funkeln, sprühen; **b)** *(perform brilliantly)* glänzen; **c)** *(be lively)* sprühen (**with** vor + *Dat.*). **2.** *n.* Glitzern, *das;* Funkeln, *das*

8 Translate the words in bold print.

JOKE

On a long bus journey, an old man was greatly irritated by a little girl sitting next to him who ***kept sniffing****.*
"Have you got a hanky[1]?" he asked her.
"Yes," she replied, "but my Mum wouldn't like me to lend it to a stranger."

1 Taschentuch

tipps&tricks

She *kept sniffing* kannst du nicht wörtlich übersetzen. Vielmehr schreibst du Sie schnupfte *andauernd*, wobei du das englische Verb *keep* im Deutschen mit dem Adverb *andauernd* wiedergibst.
Habe Mut und übersetze manchmal frei!

Go on.

a) **Go on** reading, Peter. You're doing well.
b) I **like** playing the piano, but I **dislike** washing up.
c) What do you **prefer**: school or holidays?
d) Susan **is likely to** win the match.
e) The story **seems to** be boring; everyone is yawning.
f) My grandparents **used to** live in that house.
g) We **hope to** see you soon.
h) I **happened to** meet an old friend.
i) It **may** rain this afternoon. We'd better take an umbrella.
j) I **suppose** I've forgotten something.

Choose between:

wahrscheinlich · *weiter* · *anscheinend* · *hoffentlich* · *vermutlich* · *früher* · *lieber* · *zufällig* · *gern* · *ungern* · *vielleicht*

9 Translate.

a) How long *have you been* ill, Sharon?
   – *I have been* ill since Saturday.

b) How long *have you been learning* English, Jason?
   – *I have been learning* it for five years now.

c) What are your plans for the summer holidays, Brian?
   – I'*ll go* to Brighton in August.
   – *I'm going to attend* a course for advanced learners.

d) What *is Jane doing*?
   – She *is sitting* in her room and *reading* a magazine.
   What *were you doing* at ten o'clock last night, Bill?
   – I *was watching* the soccer match on TV.

e) After *he had done* his homework, Jason *went* to see his friends.

tipps&tricks In manchen Fällen solltest du Zeiten etwas freier übersetzen, z. B. bei a) und b) Hier wäre das Präsens (mit schon) für *present perfect* bzw. *present perfect progressive* vorzuziehen. c) Mit dem Präsens kannst du hier englisches *future* übersetzen, v. a. wenn eine Zeitangabe dabeisteht. d) Die Verlaufsform kannst du mit gerade ausdrücken. e) Die Zeitenfolge *(past perfect* und *simple past)* gibst du genau wieder.

10 Mind the tenses.

a) Has the bus arrived yet?
   – No, it hasn't come yet.

b) How long has Jane had this bike?
   – She's had it for one year.

c) How long has Mrs Miller been working as a secretary?
   – For five years.

d) How long have you known the Millers?
   – For over two years.

e) What are you going to do in your summer holidays?
   – We're going to play tennis and go swimming.

f) Tony was very tired because he hadn't slept for two nights.

11 Translate the words in bold print.

JOKE

Dad was in a terrible temper over his son's latest school report.
"It says here that you became bottom in a class of twenty-four," he shouted.
"That's dreadful!"
***"It might be** worse, Dad," said the boy.*
***"There might have been** more kids in the class."*

Go on.

a) We needn't take an umbrella.
   We mustn't forget the key.
b) May we park our car here?
   You can park it over there.
c) I may be wrong.
   I may have been wrong.
d) We might find the key.
   We might have lost the key in the garden.
e) We ought to do something.
   We ought to have come earlier.
f) You shouldn't leave the door open, Paul.
   You shouldn't have left the window open, girls.

tipps&tricks

Bei den Modalverben solltest du die Bedeutungsunterschiede stets klar herausstellen, z. B.
must not (nicht dürfen)
need not (nicht zu brauchen)
may (dürfen; vielleicht sein)
should + *ought to* (sollte,n)

12 **Translate.**

a) *Taking* part in a marathon means more than just running.

. . . .

b) *Watching* a detective film is great fun.

. . . .

tipps&tricks

Eine -ing-Form kann Subjekt eines Satzes sein und wird im Deutschen oft mit einem Infinitiv oder frei wiedergegeben, z. B. a) An einem Marathonlauf *teilzunehmen .../Die Teilnahme* an einem Marathonlauf.

c) Jason enjoys *watching* detective films.

. . . .

d) His girl friend loves *playing* the piano.

. . . .

tipps&tricks

Eine -ing-Form (nach bestimmten Verben) übersetzt du ebenfalls oft mit einem Infinitiv, z. B. c) Es macht Jason Spaß, ... *anzuschauen,* oder mit einem Adverb, z. B. d) Sie ... *sehr gerne*.

e) It's no use *waiting* any longer. Let's go.

. . . .

f) Paul succeeded *in passing* his driving test.

. . . .

g) Jane is crazy about *playing* baseball.

. . . .

tipps&tricks

Die -ing-Form (nach Wendungen, Verben + Präpositionen, Adjektiv + Präposition) übersetzt du häufig mit einem Infinitiv, z. B. e) Es hat keinen Zweck, ... *zu warten*.

13 **Translate.**

a) Youngsters *working for the community* take no jobs away from adults.

. . . .

b) There was complete silence *broken only by a train*.

. . . .

tipps&tricks

Diese Partizipien entsprechen einem *Relativsatz*. Wenn du dir das klarmachst, fällt dir die Übersetzung leichter, z. B. a) Youngsters *who are* working, b) silence *which was* broken.

c) *Feeling* very tired, Jason went straight to bed.

. . . .

d) *Before going* to her office, Mrs Clarke has a decent breakfast.

. . . .

e) *Seeing* that it was already half past eight, Mrs Clarke hurried to the bus stop.

. . . .

tipps&tricks

Partizipien können auch anstelle eines Nebensatzes verwendet werden. Bei c) ist es ein Nebensatz des Grundes: *As he felt very tired, ...* ; bei d) und e) sind es Nebensätze der Zeit: *Before she went ...* bzw. *When she saw that ...*

JOKE

A murderer ***sitting*** *in the electric chair was about to be executed. "Have you any last request?" asked the prison chaplain. "Yes", replied the killer. "Will you hold my hand?"*

14 **Translate.**

JOKE

Customer: *"This restaurant must have a very clean kitchen."*
Manager: *"Thank you, Sir.* ***What makes you say that****?"*
Customer: *"Everything tastes of soap."*

a) Billy was the first to leave the classroom when he heard the bell. Andrew didn't know where to go. He had lost his timetable.

. . . .

. . . .

b) What do you want me to do, Paul? I'd like you to help me with this article.

. . . .

. . . .

tipps&tricks

Auch bei Infinitivkonstruktionen musst du oft eine freie Übersetzung versuchen, z. B. make sb. do sth. (*jemanden dazu bringen*, etwas zu tun), a) Billy war der erste, *der ... verließ* bzw. Andrew wusste nicht, *wohin er ... sollte*, b) Was *willst* du, *dass ... ich mache* bzw. *Ich möchte, dass du ...* .

15 **Go on.**

a) Do you know how to draw an elephant, Billy?
b) Jane doesn't know where to sit.
c) We can't expect Susan to wait any longer.
d) Jack wants his parents to give him their car.
e) There is no reason for Tom to leave earlier.
f) All the pupils waited for Mr Penner to finish his lesson.
g) The detective film made me cry.
h) We had better stay at home next Friday.

advice	Rat
advise	raten, beraten
according to	nach, laut
airliner	Verkehrsflugzeug
apply for	sich um etwas bewerben
apply to	sich bei jemandem bewerben
argue	streiten, diskutieren
attend	besuchen, anwesend sein
avoid	vermeiden
Austria	Österreich
beyond	jenseits
biro	Kugelschreiber
blame	jemandem die Schuld geben
busker	Straßenmusikant
calculator	Rechenmaschine
choice	Auswahl
commercial	Werbespot
community centre	Gemeindezentrum
consumer	Verbraucher(in)
crane	Kran
cub	(Bären-)Junges
deaf	taub
deal in	mit etwas handeln
deal with	von etwas handeln
develop	entwickeln
disagree	nicht übereinstimmen
disagreement	Meinungsverschiedenheit
destroy	zerstören
efficient	tüchtig, rationell
employer	Arbeitgeber(in)
employee	Arbeitnehmer(in)
encourage	ermutigen
expect	erwarten
environment	Umgebung, Umwelt
famous	berühmt
forbid	verbieten
frequent	häufig

guide	Führer(in)
gradual	allmählich
gymnasium	Turnhalle
improve	verbessern
income	Einkommen
inexpensive	billig, preisgünstig
increase	erhöhen, zunehmen
insist on	auf etwas bestehen
likely	wahrscheinlich
low	niedrig
mean	geizig, gemein
mention	erwähnen
misery	Elend, Not
monkey	Affe
mud	Schlamm
narrow	eng
note	Notiz, Schein
notice	bemerken
novel	Roman
nurse	Krankenschwester/pfleger
occasional	gelegentlich
opponent	Gegner(in)
pedestrian	Fußgänger
pedestrian zone	Fußgängerzone
persuade	überreden
poison	Gift
poverty	Armut
print	drucken
pronounce	aussprechen
pronunciation	Aussprache
purchase	erwerben, kaufen
recognize	erkennen
refuse	ablehnen, verweigern
remove	entfernen, beseitigen
rubber	Gummi

rude	unhöflich
sail	Segel
sale	Verkauf, Ausverkauf
solution	Lösung
solve	lösen
suffer from	leiden unter
sufficient	ausreichend
suggest	vorschlagen, hindeuten auf
survive	überleben
take-off	Start (eines Flugzeugs)
tramp	Landstreicher(in)
typist	Schreibkraft
ugly	hässlich
unbeatable	unschlagbar
unlikely	unwahrscheinlich
upset	mitgenommen, bestürzt, betrübt
urge	drängen, dringend raten
vacant	frei, leer stehend
valid	gültig
valuable	wertvoll, kostbar
vary	unterschiedlich sein, schwanken
vast	riesig, riesengroß
view	Sicht, Aussicht
viewer	Fernsehzuschauer(in)
visible	sichtbar
vocational training	Berufsausbildung
wage	Lohn
warehouse	Lagerhaus, Lager
weak	schwach
welfare services	Wohlfahrtswesen
wind [ai]	(Uhr) aufziehen
wrap	einwickeln, einpacken
yawn	gähnen
Zip code	Postleitzahl (AE)

Teste deine Kenntnisse

Comprehension Test

California – The Broken Dream (S. 6–12)

1. ... is the second largest city in the U.S.A.
2. ... it did terrible damage.
3. ... an earthquake destroyed San Francisco.
4. ... the state cannot (afford to) support and educate them.
5. life
6. dead
7. description
8. loss
9. nightmare/catastrophe/disaster
10. shared
11. squeezed
12. economy
13. ... in the morning
14. There is a lot of/very dense traffic on the highways of L.A.
15. ... badly hurt
16. ... particularly rich
17. ... because of/as a result of
18. ... a (very) bad/horrible dream.
19. ... people who leave their home countries and settle somewhere else/
    ... people who want to live in another country.
    ... foreigners who come into a country to settle/begin a new life there.
20. Her bed moved around the room, and a picture flew off the wall.
21. It was a public holiday.
22. (The map shows that) the San Andreas Fault (line) is not far away.
    (The text says that) scientists are expecting another big quake in California.
23. The economy in California has suffered. Too many immigrants come from Asia and Latin America.
    Many people are unemployed. There are a lot of race problems in California.
24. I would like to travel to Florida because the weather there is warm and nice all year round. I think visiting Disney World would be great fun.
25. Sometimes there is too much snow in southern Germany. In winter/spring 1994 a lot of heavy snow fell. Branches and trees broke, which caused a lot of damage in our forests./We had no electricity because electric wires had broken under the snow. or: Sometimes there are heavy rainfalls, and rivers, like the Rhine, have too much water. Streets and buildings are under water, and the fire brigade must be called to pump the water out of basements/help people who are in danger.

26. After football matches groups of fans/hooligans, who are usually drunk, march through the streets, smash windows/fight. Fans must be checked carefully before the match starts, so that they cannot take any dangerous objects with them.
27. have been living (have lived)/of/slightly/are (being) taught/to react/occurs/be done/have been worked out/himself/who/could forecast/are going to stay (will stay)/to spending/in (of)/was built/latest/costs/would have survived/ more careful/too
28. - I left Frankfurt at 5 p.m./in the afternoon, on July 31.
    - Martin was waiting for me at San Francisco airport, (when) I arrived at 10 o'clock at night.
    - He took me/we drove to Stanford, where I stayed with him on the university campus.
    - On the (following) weekend we travel(l)ed/drove/went/made a trip to San Francisco, which is about 40 miles away.
    - It/the weather was (rather) cool; the temperature reached only 18°C.
    - We bought a few souvenirs and spent the night in a motel.
29. You should have/prepare a first aid box kit so that you can help/assist injured people.
    Prepare/store some (canned) food and water because getting food after an earthquake may be difficult/impossible.
    Hide/lie under a table/desk because things/heavy objects may fall on your head/you are protected from falling objects.
    Don't light a match/fire because the flames may spread quickly/an explosion can take place.
    Listen to the news. It may give you information/advice about what to do next/where to get help.
    Don't drive/use your car. Roads and bridges might be destroyed/you must keep roads clear for ambulances.

30. **Translate into German:** **(S. 13)**
    Die Richterskala zeigt an, wie groß ein Erdbeben ist, und die Auswirkungen, die es haben kann. Schon kleinen Kindern in Kalifornien wird folgendes gesagt:
    Das Beben ist so leicht, dass man es kaum bemerken/wahrnehmen kann.
    Häuser beben, als ob schwere Lastwagen vorbeifahren. Die Leute wachen auf und die Kirchenglocken läuten.
    Bäume fangen zu schwingen an. Lose/Lockere Gegenstände fallen aus den Regalen.
    Ein allgemeiner Alarm geht los/wird ausgelöst. Mauern und Decken werden beschädigt. Gasleitungen explodieren. Kamine und Außenwände stürzen ein.

Züge entgleisen. Brücken und hohe Gebäude sind zerstört, wenn sie nicht ordentlich gebaut wurden.
Feuer brechen aus und können Menschen töten. Städte liegen in Schutt und Asche/Ruinen.
Die Erdoberfläche bewegt sich in steigenden und fallenden Wellen, was zur völligen Zerstörung führt/was die völlige Zerstörung verursacht.

1.1 Eine Textstelle finden (S. 14/15)

1. a) A Scotsman went to see his doctor.
   b) You will lose your sight.
   c) He felt no better.
   d) I've seen about all that's worth seeing.

2. a) ... there was no vacant seat on the bus.
   b) ... the woman entered.
   c) ... forced him back.
   d) ... offer her a seat.

1.2 Richtig oder falsch? (S. 16–18)

3. a) T b) F c) F d) T e) T f) F
4. a) T b) F c) T d) F e) F f) T g) F h) F
5. a) false ... at this time of the year (d.h. Christmas)
   b) true ... twice as many as in 1980
   c) false ... the churches we use as temporary shelters
   d) false ... the churches are too small
   e) true ... they will be provided with the services of hairdressers.

1.3 Fragen zum Text (S. 19–22)

6. a) She lives in Australia.
   b) She got married in 1981.
   c) Her youngest child is six.
   d) The air fare was too expensive.
   e) No, she wasn't. She became very frightened.
   f) He said that not a single air-mail letter to their daughter had been lost on the way.

7. a) They are used on modern building sites.
   b) He dropped his hammer in the cement mixer.
   c) They tried to fish it out with a long pair of tongs.
   d) The mechanism was broken and there were no spare parts available.
   e) The firm lost thousands of pounds.
   f) He was careless.
   g) He threw the hammer back into the cement mixer.

8. a) He thought it would not be healthy because there was no fresh water near it.
   b) He thought four things were necessary.
   c) He would need fresh water.
   d) He wanted to see any ship that came near the island.
   e) He was going to pitch his tent on it.
   f) He had taken them from the ship.

9. a) It is called the White House.
   b) It is in Washington, DC.
   c) They can visit the White House from Tuesday to Saturday.
   d) Tickets are valid only on the day when they are sold.
   e) Tickets may be gone as early as half past eight.

1.4 Eine Meinung vertreten. (S. 25–27)

10. a) I agree because men look more elegant wearing ties with a suit, especially if they have to deal with customers./I disagree. Often men feel uncomfortable in a suit with a shirt and a tie. They may not be very nice to their customers then.
    b) I agree because girls usually have slim legs and small feet, which makes Docs look ridiculous./I don't think so. They look quite good under a long skirt or with trousers. The leather is so soft that they aren't heavy at all.
    c) I agree because I live in a country where people can say what they like. There is freedom of speech./I don't agree with that. We shouldn't hurt other people's feelings, for instance with radical slogans.

11. I'd like to visit London because there I could see a lot of famous sights, such as the Tower or Buckingham Palace. I'd also go to Scotland because I like hiking in the mountains.

12. They come to London because of the sights or museums. Some want to practise their English, and others want to see a musical in one of London's famous theatres.

13. The advantage is that an underground is quicker. Traffic jams can be avoided.

14. Fast food is quick and convenient. But it is also quite expensive and not always healthy.

15. I'd like to visit Florida. There are marvellous beaches, and the weather is warm all year round.

2.1 Synonyme (S. 30–31)

1. a) punctually b) enough c) to want d) before e) to reach f) by car.

2. a) possess b) buy c) enough d) boring e) convince f) happy g) permit h) destroy i) draw j) complete k) receive l) almost m) perfect n) repair o) kinds p) precious q) answer r) large

2.2 Umschreibungen (S. 32–36)

3. a) They can go in without paying b) Tickets can be bought/You can buy tickets c) write to/ring up/contact/get in touch with d) apart from.

4. a) 2 b) 3 c) 6 d) 5 e) 9 f) 10 g) 1 h) 4 i) 7 j) 8.

5. a) 3 b) 6 c) 2 d) 5 e) 9 f) 8 g) 1 h) 10 i) 7 j) 4.

6. a) They are in another country. b) She can't see. c) You can rely on her (work). d) She asked them to come. e) He takes care of her. f) He hasn't enough money (to buy it). g) She let it fall. (let, let, let!).

7. while: a) I met my uncle while I was in London. b) I waited a long while.
   change: a) I want to play soccer, so I must change my clothes. b) There's been a change in the weather.
   way: a) Can you show me the way out? b) I like the American way of life.

8. a) fine: We had fine weather. The driver will have to pay a fine.
   b) fit: Tom keeps fit by jogging. These shoes don't fit.

2.3 Definitionen (S. 37–40)

9. a) museum ... beautiful paintings. b) church ... where many kings and queens are buried. c) large department store ... almost everything.

10. a) ... a room where ... 5; b) ... a building where ... 1; c) a place where ... 6; d) ... a place where 7; e) ... a building where ... 10; f) ... a park where ... 2; g) ... a place along a road where ... 9; h) ... a place where ... 4; i) ... a house where ... 8; j) ... a place where ... 3.

11. a) ... an especially heavy and high shoe. b) ... soft wet earth. c) ... made from the skin of an animal. d) ... used for the wheels of motorcars.

12. a) A by-pass is ... 8; b) 4 c) 1 d) 6 e) 9 f) 2 g) 10 h) 7 i) 3 j) 5.

13. a) ... teaches, especially in schools. b) ... who is being taught at school or privately. c) ... are very popular. d) ... pupils are taught. e) ... you can carry your books. f) ... you and your teacher write on the board.

14. a) ... who ... 5; b) ... who ...10; c) ... who ... 6; d) ... who ... 8; e) ... who ... 1; f) ... who ... 4; g) ... who ... 9; h) ... who ... 3; i) ... who ... 2; j) ... who ... 7.

15. a) ... is ... 6; b) ... is ... 10; c) ... is ... 8; d) ... is ... 9; e) ... is ... 7; f) ... is ... 5; g) ... is ... 1; h) ... is ... 2; i) ... is ... 3; j) ... is ... 4.

2.4 Wörter mit entgegengesetzter Bedeutung (S. 41–44)

16. a) boring b) quickly/fast c) down d) little.

17. a) love b) whisper c) import d) forget e) answer f) win g) distribute h) succeed i) take j) end k) attack l) close m) lend n) buy o) permit. – OPPOSITE – ANTONYM

18. a) 10; b) 5; c) 12; d) 6; e) 1; f) 7; g) 2; h) 8; i) 3; j) 9; k) 4; l) 11.

19. a) 6; b) 11; c) 10; d) 9; e) 2; f) 12; g) 1; h) 4; i) 3; j) 5; k) 7; l) 8.

20. a) unhappy/sad b) unload (to unload = Infinitiv!) c) disagree d) irregular e) disadvantage f) useless.

2.5 Wortfamilien (S. 46–48)

21. a) politician b) popularity c) explanation d) drawing e) refusal.

22. a) footballer b) beginning c) successful d) congratulated e) attraction.

23. a) pianist b) musician c) builder d) teacher e) typist f) kidnapper g) beggars h) visitors.

24. a) building b) calculator(s) c) discussion d) drawing e) knowledge f) meaning g) crowded h) noisy i) angry j) valuable k) lucky, wonderful l) changeable m) application n) argument o) choice p) destruction q) failure r) loss s) qualification t) recognition u) reduction v) sale w) solution x) weight.

2.6 Arbeit mit dem Lexikon (S. 50–53)

25. a) to meet b) known c) have no pity d) to see a particular side e) have no knowledge f) expert.

26. a) Freizeit, (Weltraum) Zeitalter b) Raumschiff, Weltraum, Raumfahrer, Spaziergang im All c) (ein Platz) frei d) Ersatzrad e) Gästezimmer f) innerhalb einer Stunde.

27. a) das weite flache Land b) weitläufig c) Spanier d) ein schlauer Kopf.

3.1 Vermischte Grammatik (S. 54–60)

1. a) was listening/listened b) from c) Spanish, had just finished d) turned, Austrian, was playing e) better f) was, needed to make g) enjoyed making, did not like h) dressed/who were dressed, beautiful, extremely well i) themselves j) had not started to rain.

2. a) is suffering from, has grown b) is expected, to build c) poisoning, will change, drastically d) die e) lower, have been ignored f) of controlling g) most efficient.

3. a) worked, clear, working b) has increased, sharing, had to, spend/are spending, still do not share/are still not sharing, cooking, said/have said, stayed, probably, must be solved, will decide.

4. a) who, flight, nervous, on, before b) won't you, anxiously c) anyone d) on, for, who, uneasy e) than.

5. a) myself, such as (wie etwa), nor (neither ... nor) b) who/whom/ — (Objektfall!), — (to wonder = sich fragen), one c) either (not ... either), on, by d) at, on, between
e) — (to remember = sich erinnern an), won't you, will.

3.2 Die Zeiten im Aktiv und Passiv (S. 61–62)

6. a) is ... doing, is watching, watches b) did ... miss, fell off, broke, had to c) has changed, have been built, has not been finished d) has just passed, will be, will allow.

7. a) must be repaired, will be repaired b) have you been learning, have been learning c) did you travel, was d) is, is, will be e) was, were injured, had to be taken
f) Have (you) ever been, (I) haven't, (I) have already made, (I) am going to fly
g) were (you) doing, (I) was watching, scored, won.

3.3 If-Sätze (S. 64–65)

8. a) will stay, can't go b) would travel, could see, might meet c) would have walked, might have been

9. a) would buy (could = past!) b) were c) had not rained d) doesn't come e) don't phone f) would have lost g) water h) don't improve i) would be j) would have worn.

3.4 -ing-Form oder to-Infinitiv (S. 66–67)

10. to see, of going, (in) getting, queueing.

11. a) to attend, sitting b) for being, to come c) to travelling, to see d) getting, of sleeping e) in passing, on driving f) by selling, working g) having, waiting h) to be, making.

3.5 Objekt + to-Infinitiv (S. 70–71)

12. a) Jason to become, him to go b) for his parents to persuade, for them to change, for me to make.

13. a) their teacher to give b) Andy to stay out, him to be c) his pupils to work, them to do d) me to write, you to do e) for me to help f) for the police to come g) for us to swim h) for Jane to make.

3.6 Adjektiv – Adverb (S. 72–73)

14. a) sadly, bitterly b) immediately c) rude, totally upset, ugly d) kindly, nice e) good, awfully nice.

15. a) really good b) correctly c) awfully bad d) heavily e) hard, difficult f) extremely unfair g) easy, more difficult h) better, best i) more expensive, cheaper j) absolutely boring, most boring.

3.7 Indirekte Rede (S. 74)

16. a) ... why he had been absent from school the day before. b) he hadn't been well, he had had a bit of a temperature. c) if he had a note from his mother or his father. d) that he didn't have such a thing. e) that she would expect to see one the following day. f) to bring one. g) had been absent from school because of a cold.

3.8 Partizip-Sätze (S. 76)

17. a) ... the travellers who were waiting ... b) ... complete silence which/that was broken ... c) After he had done ... d) As she felt it would be ... e) ... and hoped to get help. f) a little girl who was sitting ... g) ... because he wanted to give him ... h) a game which/that is played ... .

4.1 Gelenkter Text (S. 78–80)

1. a) (This means) there are baths/showers. b) You can watch television. c) (The hotel) has a car park. d) (You are not) allowed to bring your dog.

2. Yesterday I was walking along Park Lane when I saw an old lady (who was) carrying a big bag. I went up to her and asked: "Excuse me, may/can I help you with your bag?" "Oh, thank you very much," the old lady replied, "you are a very polite young man." I carried the bag to her house and she said: "Thanks again." "You're welcome," I answered and went on my way.

3. The man is preparing the dinner for his wife and taking care of the twins. Unfortunately, the children are screaming because they have thrown their toys out and want them back. The dinner is burning, and the poor man is having a terrible time! He is now telephoning his wife to come to help him.

The message of this is "Don't panic!" It suggests men can't look after the home/can't cope with housework and children.

4.2 Lückendialog (S. 81–83)

4. a) Have you seen it? b) What's it like/What sort of film is it? c) Who/What is it about? d) Let's go and see it. e) ... I have to be home soon. f) What/How about tomorrow evening? g) ... I can't come tomorrow ... there's a meeting in our tennis club/oder anderer Grund!

5. a) Hello. This is Jane. Who's speaking, please? b) How are you, Paul? c) What are you doing? d) Is it easy? e) Will you finish it by four o'clock? f) Can we meet at the café then? g) Can we meet at the weekend? h) What time would you/do you suggest? i) Shall I pick you up in the car? j) How much time will you have? k) Okay. Bye.

6. a) What's your job? b) Where do you live? c) Is it far from the town centre? d) How do you get to your office? e) Do you like your job? f) What time/When do you start work? g) What does your husband do/What's your husband's job? h) Have you got any children? i) How old are they? j) Okay/You're welcome. Good-bye.

4.3 Gelenkter Dialog (S. 85–87)

7. a) What's wrong with you/What's the matter with you? b) I've had a cough for months now and I can't get rid of it. c) Do you smoke heavily? d) Yes, I do. I usually smoke five or ten cigarettes a day, but now and then/sometimes even as many as fifteen. e) Do you realise that smoking is extremely unhealthy? f) I don't mind. I'm still young. g) Have you ever tried to give up smoking? h) I've tried it twice, but I haven't managed it yet.

8. a) Hello, Jeff. b) Hello, Ian. I haven't seen you for quite some time. c) Where did you spend your last holidays? d) First I was in Wales and then I flew to Canada. Shall I show you some photos? e) Oh, yes. I'd like very much to see them. When could we meet? f) Well/Let me see. The best day would be next Saturday at six p.m. at my house. g) Can I bring my sister with me? She is very interested in Canada. h) Yes, of course. I look forward/I'm looking forward to our meeting.

9. a) T.A.: "What can I do for you?"
W.: I'm planning a journey to the Continent.
b) T.A.: The shortest way would be from Manchester to Hull.

W.: Is there a ferry from Hull to the Continent?

c) T.A.: Yes, there is. The ferry leaves at 6 p.m. and goes directly to Ostend or Rotterdam.

W.: I'd prefer Ostend because we could visit Brussels. How much is the ferry for two people and a car?

d) T.A.: The single fare including a cabin is about £ 180

W.: This route would be best for us because we needn't go by car through all of England. Do we have to book the ferry in advance in August?

e) T.A.: Yes, of course. It's necessary because a lot of people travel in this month.

W.: I'm going to book a return and I'll like to pay the tickets right now.

f) T.A.: Thank you very much. Have a nice holiday.

4.4 Brief schreiben (S. 90–92)

10. Dear Susan, ... Maria Klein, ... Neustadt, ... to tell you something about myself, ... riding and knitting, swimming, ... a farmer, ... is a secretary, ... Neuburg, ... thirty-two pupils, ... 7.50 a.m. ... 12.35 p.m., Saturday, ... hear from you soon, ... best wishes, Yours Maria.

11. Dear Gabi, I've been here in London for three days now. The weather is beautiful. I've visited the Tower, Hyde Park and Big Ben. The ferry to Ostend will leave on Saturday. I'm looking forward to seeing you soon. Lots of love, Peter.

12. Dear Mrs Ashton. I want/would like to be an au-pair girl in England. I got your address from an advertisement in the "Stuttgarter Zeitung" last Saturday. I left secondary school at sixteen. I was employed at a kindergarten for one year. Then I did another year at technical high school. I visited England last year, and I would like to spend a longer time there in order to improve my English. After that year I intend to study social science. I hope to receive a reply soon. Yours sincerely, Susanne Meister.

5. Übersetzung (S. 94)

1. Nun bist du der stolze Besitzer von einem Paar Qualitätsschuhen. Durch den Kauf von Dr. Martens (Schuhen) hast du die richtige Wahl getroffen. Sie werden von Jung und Alt getragen, von Bankiers ebenso wie von Polizisten, von Rockstars und Krankenschwestern. Sie halten sehr lange und sind das ganze Jahr über modisch.

Natürlich sind unsere Schuhe und Stiefel immer wieder nachgemacht worden. Diese Nachahmungen sehen ähnlich aus; erst wenn man sie trägt, wird einem klar, dass sie nicht dasselbe sind. Du wirst bald herausfinden, wie gut die wirklichen „Doc Martens“ deine Füße vor Kälte, Schmutz und Schnee schützen. Ihr weiches Leder und ihre dicken Gummisohlen sind unschlagbar. Obwohl es leicht ist, deine „Doc Martens“ zu schonen, solltest du die darunterstehende Gebrauchsanweisung befolgen: Entferne Schmutz mit einem feuchten Tuch. Trage gelegentlich Schuhcreme oder Wachs auf, und deine Schuhe werden so gut aussehen wie am ersten Tag.

5.1 Unbekannte Wörter erschließen (S. 96–97)

2. (er) rief aus; Ausgänge.

3. a) ausdrücken b) ausführen c) äußerst d) außerordentlich e) Ausgaben, Kosten (expensive = teuer!) f) Ausstellung g) Schüleraustausch h) ausgezeichnet i) beeindrucken j) einführen k) Einwohner l) einwandern m) Einwanderung n) Einwanderer.

4. a) unsicher; b) unhöflich; c) unabhängig; d) unregelmäßig; e) unsichtbar; f) unmöglich; g) unrichtig/falsch; h) unfähig, unproduktiv; i) billig/nicht teuer; j) informell/zwanglos; k) ungewöhnlich; l) unschlagbar; m) unglaublich; n) unsicher; o) bewusstlos (!); p) unzählbar; q) sich ausziehen; r) Arbeitslosigkeit (!); s) nicht übereinstimmen mit; t) Meinungsverschiedenheit; u) Nachteil; v) unehrlich; w) nicht gehorchen; x) unzufrieden

   a) wiederverwerten/recyceln; b) noch einmal überdenken; c) wiederaufbauen; d) wiederholen/abspielen; e) wieder aufziehen (Uhr); f) neu einteilen/umorganisieren.

5.2 Falsche Freunde und schwierige Wörter (S. 98–104)

5. a) Jason will Grundschullehrer werden. b) Sarah arbeitete so schwer, dass sie schließlich krank wurde. c) Andrew sah eine Schlange an der Tür. d) Ehe Billy zur Turnhalle ging, hatte er eine Landkarte gekauft.

6. überhaupt nicht — vielleicht — a) über b) vor c) fast d) schon e) immer f) obwohl g) schließlich h) mindestens i) schon einmal/je j) jedoch k) auch nicht l) noch nicht.

7. Veränderung – a) für, seit, um ... nachzuschlagen, nach, gegen, wegen b) vorbei (go by = vergehen), bis spätestens, von, indem ... schrieb, mit dem, am c) auf, an, mit dem, zu (Fuß), als (... erhielt), im (Fernsehen), bei (mir), los (Was ist los?), weiter d) Weg, (this way) hierher, Art, Methode/Art, (a long way) weit, Richtung, (give way to) ... hat Vorfahrt, andersherum, Lebensweise e) meinst, bedeutet, Bedeutungen, es sollte sein, gemein, Verkehrsmittel f) verwende(t), (used to live) lebte früher, ich bin es nicht gewohnt, Benutzung/Einsatz, Zweck, es hat keinen Zweck g) Frei(zeit), Ersatz(rad), Hast du ... Zeit für mich?

8. (sie) schnupfte andauernd – a) (Lies) weiter b) gern, ungern c) hast du lieber d) (gewinnt) wahrscheinlich e) (ist) anscheinend f) (lebten) früher g) hoffentlich h) (traf) zufällig i) (es regnet) vielleicht j) vermutlich.

5.3 Zeiten übersetzen (S. 105)

9. a) Wie lange bist du schon krank, Sharon? Ich bin schon seit Samstag krank. b) Wie lange lernst du schon Englisch, Jason? Ich lerne es nun schon seit fünf Jahren. c) Welche Pläne hast du für die Sommerferien, Brian? Im August fahre ich nach Brighton. Ich besuche einen Kurs für Fortgeschrittene. d) Was macht Jane gerade? Sie sitzt in ihrem Zimmer und liest eine Zeitschrift. Was hast du gestern Abend um 10 Uhr gemacht, Bill? Ich habe mir das Fußballspiel im Fernsehen angeschaut. e) Nachdem er seine Hausaufgabe gemacht hatte, besuchte Jason seine Freunde.

10. a) Ist der Bus schon gekommen? Nein, er ist noch nicht da. b) Wie lange hat Jane dieses Rad/das Rad hier schon? Sie hat es seit einem Jahr. c) Wie lange arbeitet Frau Miller schon als Sekretärin? Seit fünf Jahren. d) Wie lange kennst du/kennt ihr die Millers schon? Seit über zwei Jahren. e) Was machst du in deinen Sommerferien/Was wirst du ... machen? Wir werden Tennis spielen und zum Baden gehen. f) Tony war sehr müde, weil er zwei Nächte lang nicht geschlafen hatte.

5.4 Modalverben (S. 106)

11. Es könnte (schlimmer) sein, (In der Klasse) hätten (mehr Kinder) sein können. – a) Wir brauchen keinen Schirm mitzunehmen. Wir dürfen den Schlüssel nicht vergessen. b) Dürfen wir unser Auto hier parken? Ihr dürft/könnt es dort drüben parken. c) Vielleicht habe ich Unrecht. Vielleicht habe ich Unrecht gehabt. d) Vielleicht finden wir den Schlüssel. Vielleicht

haben wir den Schlüssel im Garten verloren/Wir könnten ... verloren haben. e) Wir sollten etwas unternehmen/tun. Wir hätten früher kommen sollen. f) Du solltest die Tür nicht offen lassen, Paul. Ihr hättet das Fenster nicht offen lassen sollen, Mädchen.

5.5 Schwierige Konstruktionen (S. 107–108)

12. a) An einem Marathonlauf teilzunehmen/Die Teilnahme an einem Marathonlauf bedeutet mehr als nur zu laufen. b) Einen Krimi anzuschauen macht viel Spaß. c) Es macht Jason Spaß, Krimis anzuschauen/Jason schaut gerne ... an. d) Seine Freundin spielt sehr gerne Klavier. e) Es hat keinen Zweck, länger zu warten. Lasst uns gehen. f) Paul gelang es, seine Fahrprüfung zu bestehen. g) Jane ist verrückt/ganz wild darauf, Baseball zu spielen.

13. a) Jugendliche, die für die Allgemeinheit arbeiten, nehmen Erwachsenen keine Arbeitsplätze weg. b) Es herrschte (eine) völlige Stille, die nur von einem Zug unterbrochen wurde. c) Da er sich sehr müde fühlte, ging Jason geradewegs ins Bett. d) Ehe sie in ihr Büro geht/fährt, genehmigt sich Frau Clarke ein anständiges Frühstück. e) Als sie sah, dass es schon halb neun war, eilte Frau Clarke zur Bushaltestelle.

14. Was bringt sie dazu, das zu sagen/Was veranlasst sie, das zu sagen? a) Billy war der erste, der das Klassenzimmer verließ, als er die Glocke hörte. Andrew wusste nicht, wo er hingehen sollte. Er hatte seinen Stundenplan verloren. b) Was willst du, dass ich mache, Paul? Ich möchte, dass du mir bei diesem Artikel hilfst.

15. a) Weißt du, wie man einen Elefanten zeichnet, Billy? b) Jane weiß nicht, wo sie sich hinsetzen soll. c) Wir können nicht erwarten, dass Susan länger wartet. d) Jack will/möchte, dass seine Eltern ihm das Auto geben. e) Es gibt keinen Grund für Tom, früher zu gehen. f) Alle Schüler warteten darauf, dass Herr Penner seine Stunde beendet. g) Der Krimi brachte mich zum Weinen. h) Es wäre besser, wenn wir am nächsten Freitag zu Hause bleiben.